IN SEARCH OF
PHARRELL WILLIAMS

PAUL LESTER

IN SEARCH OF PHARRELL WILLIAMS

PAUL LESTER

OMNIBUS PRESS

London / New York / Paris / Sydney / Copenhagen / Berlin / Madrid / Tokyo

Copyright © 2015 Omnibus Press
(A Division of Music Sales Limited)

Cover designed by Ruth Keating.
Picture research: Sarah Bacon.

ISBN: 978.1.78305.789.4
Order No: OP56210

Exclusive Distributors
Music Sales Limited,
14/15 Berners Street,
London, W1T 3LJ.

Music Sales Corporation,
180 Madison Avenue, 24th Floor,
New York NY 10016, USA.

Macmillan Distribution Services,
56 Parkwest Drive
Derrimut, Vic 3030,
Australia.

Printed in the EU.

A catalogue record for this book is available from the British Library.

Visit Omnibus Press on the web at www.omnibuspress.com

Contents

Acknowledgements

I was fortunate to be able to spend the day with Pharrell Williams, and interview him at length, in February 2004. This book includes previously unpublished material from that encounter. There is also unpublished material from my interviews with Nile Rodgers of Chic (from 2013), Tyler, The Creator (from 2011) and Earl Sweatshirt (from 2013). I am grateful to them all for their courtesy and openness.

Introduction

How good is Pharrell Williams? So good that he managed to make Ed Sheeran – previously an acoustic singer-songwriter with no little success but next to zero credibility – seem cool. With his production and co-writing of the single 'Sing', he managed to, overnight, transform the doughy ginger troubadour into a louche and lithe, Anglo answer to Justin Timberlake.

But then, Williams could get pop gold out of the basest raw material. And he was on something of a roll that year. In 2013-14, dubbed by Oprah Winfrey "The Year Of Pharrell", he was everywhere: his singles, either as a team or main player, notably Robin Thicke's 'Blurred Lines', Daft Punk's 'Get Lucky' and his own 'Happy', were the world's biggest hits. Truly, this was a golden age for the boy from Virginia Beach.

Actually, "boy" isn't quite right, and there's another reason why his colossal success was so extraordinary: he was achieving it at the relatively ripe old age of 40-plus. Historically, musicians, from Elvis Presley to Michael Jackson, The Beatles to The Beastie Boys, have done their best work in their twenties, or at a stretch their early thirties. Pharrell – and he was increasingly becoming known solely by his first name, joining that elite pantheon of mononymous pop stars that includes Madonna, Prince, Beyoncé, Rihanna and Kanye – was enjoying superstardom when most artists' popularity is on the decline.

His boyish good looks were part of the appeal. The journalist from *Vogue* magazine had a field day with her description of the irresistible, ageless musician as "Sphinx-like, with wide-set eyes, long eyelashes and a mouth that flirts with a smile… Pharrell is remarkable looking," she decided, although he was dismissive of any attempts to laud his beauty, putting his flawless skin down to "being cognisant" and washing his face with Cetaphil and cold water. Men, too, fell for his charms, even *The Guardian*'s normally hard-nosed Simon Hattenstone admiring his "cheekbones [that] you could cut diamonds on [and] skin that should belong to a 25-year-old".

He was that rarity: the backroom boy and producer – "The guy standing next to the guy," as he memorably and self-effacingly described himself to Oprah – turned charismatic frontman. He could help performers from all genres effect transitions radical enough to make their names or rescue their careers. When Justin Timberlake wanted to remodel himself after his boy-band tenure with ★N Sync had come to a natural end, who did he call? Pharrell. When Britney Spears felt it was time to morph from cute teen pop girl-next-door to fully-fledged purveyor of adult Raunch&B, who was top of her wish list? The artist formerly known as Skateboard P.

And he could shift gear just as fast himself. Pharrell is one of those artists who refuses to stand still. His productions as one half of The Neptunes (the name for his studio partnership with Chad Hugo) have tended to change according to who is in front of the recording studio controls. His band N★E★R★D flit effortlessly between hard rock, jazz-pop and ethereal soul. His solo output makes a virtue of rampant stylistic promiscuity. The run of form that he evinced between 2013 and '14 proved that.

Even more extraordinary was that Pharrell's 2010s mastery of the charts wasn't his first moment in the sun. Far from it. He had enjoyed staggering success a full decade earlier, by which time he was already "ancient" in pop terms. That's when, in his thirties, he designed a series of innovative smash hits for Nelly ('Hot In Herre'), Britney Spears ('I'm A Slave 4 U'), Justin Timberlake ('Like I Love You'), Snoop Dogg ('Drop It Like It's Hot'), Gwen Stefani ('Hollaback Girl'), Jay-Z ('I Just Wanna Love U (Give It 2 Me)'), Mystikal ('Shake Ya Ass'), Busta Rhymes ('Pass The Courvoisier Pt. 2'), Usher ('U Don't Have To Call'), Kelis ('Milkshake') and Clipse ('Grindin'').

Pharrell and Chad Hugo were a sort of two-man Motown. Their production sorcery was so exquisitely effective that it enabled them to dominate the music scene (pop, R&B, hip hop, urban and all sectors in between). And their hegemony was so complete in the early part of the new century that all manner of mind-boggling statistics were bandied around: there was apparently a survey in August 2003 that found The Neptunes produced almost 20 percent of songs played on British radio while a similar survey in the US had them at 43 percent; they were also responsible for one-third of America's *Billboard* 100 chart.

No wonder he and Hugo were awarded the title Producer of the Decade for the 2000s by *Billboard* magazine and readers of *Vibe* magazine voted them the third greatest hip hop producers of all time, beaten only by the legendary Dr. Dre and DJ Premier. Nor is it any surprise that they were estimated to have a net worth of $155 million and, at one point, were said to be commanding as much as $150,000 to produce a single song. The Neptunes remain one of the most successful production teams in music history, with no fewer than 24 *Billboard* Hot 100 Top 10 hits during the late nineties and 2000s. In 2004, The Neptunes got the ultimate recognition for their work when they walked away with the coveted Producer of the Year award at the Grammys.

The Neptunes – so hot they were rumoured to have turned down Elton John and Mick Jagger – were the fabulous alchemical brothers for a new era. Their music was groundbreaking, even avant-garde, and yet it was also highly commercial and immaculately suited to the airwaves. In the early noughties you couldn't get through an hour of pop or rap radio without hearing their signature digital sound, with its queasily infectious blend of minimalist electronics and polyrhythmic percussion, startling use of synths and beats and guitars, their genius often a testament to what they left out of a track as much as what they put in.

Williams has long since proven that he has the Midas touch, with literally dozens of hits, whether solo or as collaborations. But his success has not just been in the pop realm. He has shown his capabilities in a variety of areas. By the 2010s he had a multimedia creative collective called i am OTHER that served as an umbrella for all of his many business endeavours including a record label (Star Trak Entertainment), apparel (his Billionaire Boys Club clothing and Ice Cream footwear brands), textiles (Bionic Yam), and a dedicated YouTube channel. He had a boutique store in New York City on West Broadway. He had co-designed a jewellery collection called Blason, spectacles for Louis Vuitton and a line of sunglasses for Moncler called Moncler Lunettes. He had worked on furniture with Emmanuel Perrotin and a French manufacturer, Domeau & Pérès. He wrote a memoir, *Places And Spaces I've Been* (with contributions from Buzz Aldrin and Jay-Z), and there was talk of authoring a series of children's books. He was named Creative Director of KarmaloopTV, "a new TV network aimed at the online generation". There was a partnership with Adidas, there were soundtrack music collaborations with Hans Zimmer, and there was his role as CEO of a non-profit organisation called From One Hand To AnOTHER whose mission it was to "change the world one kid at a time by giving them the tools and resources to meet their unique potential". He co-founded UJAM, a cloud-based music creation and production platform, announced plans to collaborate with Pritzker Prize winner Zaha Hadid on a prefab house, and he was co-owner of Brooklyn Machine Works bicycles.

How good is Pharrell Williams? He's a singer, songwriter. multi-instrumentalist, producer, philanthropist, fashion, furniture and jewellery designer, media mogul and tech guru, author and fine artist, gearhead and architect. That good.

"I'm a musician and not much more than that," he has said, with customary modesty. "Sometimes musicians say things like, 'I'm so happy they see beyond the music.' I've said it, too. But people aren't seeing beyond the music; they're seeing something in it. I'm always thinking I'm so eclectic, but the truth is that everything boils down to music for me. That's the key to my success."

CHAPTER 1

Know Who You Are

"I'm constantly pushing myself. I got that from band camp. We were pushed on a military level"

– Pharrell Williams

Pharrell Williams was born on April 5, 1973, in Virginia Beach, Virginia. There must have been something in the water, because Virginia Beach is where Tim "Timbaland" Mosley – that other chief architect of modern R&B – went to school. Missy Elliott, another preeminent rapper, songwriter and producer, was a friend of Mosley's from nearby Portsmouth while their precursor in the hi-tech urban music stakes, Teddy Riley – the New York producer and pioneer of swingbeat/New Jack Swing – relocated to Virginia Beach and built his Future Records studio there for the likes of Michael Jackson and Whitney Houston to make their groundbreaking urban music in the nineties and beyond.

His father, said to be an African-American called Pharaoh Williams II, was a handyman and house painter, and his mother,

Carolyn, was an elementary school teacher, librarian and "media specialist". A highly educated woman, she earned several degrees, one from Tidewater Community College, two from Old Dominion University and one more from Regent University, which allowed her to use the prefix "Dr." – Dr. Williams taught variously at White Oaks Elementary, Landstown Middle School, Princess Anne Middle School and Great Neck Middle School (latterly, she has also sat on the board of her son's charity From One Hand To AnOTHER, already explained on p 5).

According to some sources, before specialising in education – and a couple of years before she gave birth to Pharrell – she made the most of her good looks as a Filipina beauty queen: formerly known as Caroline Gomora Masibay, she is said to have represented the Philippines in the Miss Asia Pacific pageant, in which she came first runner-up on June 26, 1971.

"I'm often mistaken for 28-32, but I'm almost 50," she once said, aware of her youthful genes, ones that she apparently bequeathed to her eldest son, who today looks considerably younger than his years (Pharrell also appears to have acquired his mother's bone structure and skin-tone). "I'm not being facetious," she added. "I honestly don't keep up with [age]."

It is assumed that she was still in her teens when, on Labor Day 1969, the Virginia Beach native met her future husband, Pharaoh. Within four years, Pharrell was born. He was the eldest of three sons: Cato Williams, 10 years his junior, is a professional skateboarder and a part-time film student in Los Angeles, and there is a 20-year age gap between Pharrell and Psolomon, 22, who is still in Virginia and has plans to be a quantum physicist.

"I was sort of a family joke," Dr. Williams has said of the decade gap between each of her sons' births, a time lapse that enabled her to pursue her many qualifications. "Everyone would ask, 'When are you going to be done with this degree?' I just liked learning things!" Asked how she believed her eldest son, a notoriously prolific songwriter-producer and prodigiously productive entrepreneur, would describe her, she replied: "A diligent worker."

Pharrell also has two half-brothers – Pharaoh Williams III, a rising music producer, and David Williams, a furniture salesman in Delaware – and two half-sisters, Hope Williams and Carrie Parks, from his father's first marriage of nine years to Vanessa T. Williams. His upbringing was, he recalled, typically lower-middle-class and suburban, with his striking features the only thing that separated him from his peers.

"I lived in Normalville USA and I didn't look like the average kid. I was self-conscious about my eyes," he told London's *Evening Standard*. "An open mind is all I had," he went on, alluding to his parents' pay packets and the lifestyle they allowed the Williams family to lead. "I felt like my mom and dad may have lived beyond their means. When you got outstanding bills all the time, you're living beyond your means, aren't you?"

"It wasn't, like, third world poverty," David Williams told the author of this book in 2004, for an article about his superstar brother for the *Guardian* newspaper. Reminiscing about their childhood in Virginia Beach, he said with a wry smile, "Let's just say we ate a lot of pork and beans."

Discussing this formative period in his life, with specific reference to his religious beliefs, Pharrell stated on MTV that he was a Christian, even if he was never much of a regular church-goer. "I ain't been in so long, man," he admitted. "But God knows my heart. I have conversations with God a few times every day." In an interview for the 2013 autumn/winter edition of *GQ Style* magazine, Pharrell described his religious views: "On paper I'm a Christian, but really I'm a Universalist." He dismissed those who insist God doesn't exist: "It's so incredibly arrogant and pompous. It's amazing that there are people who really believe that."

Pharrell's upbringing was, by all accounts, firm but fair, with plenty of leeway, courtesy of his parents, for creative thinking and artistic endeavours. Unlike many aspiring musicians – especially hip hop artists – Williams was used to being told that anything was possible.

"My mom thought her sons could do no wrong," he said. "She lived for us. There was plenty of discipline, but we knew we were loved. My dad is a nice guy, Southern, old-fashioned. He restores cars now. My mom has just gotten her doctorate in education."

"They have their own way of doing things," Dr Williams has said of her sons, adding: "Know your child. Then move with your heart. You know your child better than anyone. You've planted certain seeds, and all you can do is nurture them as they make their way."

Despite his mother's guidance, Pharrell only earned average grades at Princess Anne High School, which specialised in programmes for gifted children. He also chose to skip college.

"I was good at music," he recalled on CBS News. "But in the other lessons I was beating on the desks and getting on the teachers' nerves. I was probably a headache and a class clown. Loved attention. Awkward."

Nevertheless, he was, in his mother's words, "really adamant about learning", and he had fond memories of his school days. Indeed, when he returned to Princess Anne for a special visit in 2014 as one of the most successful musicians and performers of the 21st century, he had only positive things to say about his alma mater.

"My teachers here kept telling me I could [succeed]," he told reporters. "They didn't give up on me. I was the guy who was sent to the principal's office, but I was encouraged. That's the kind of diligence we need. That's why teachers should be paid more. That tender loving care led me to this place. "Life," he added, "is like a mosaic. It's a bunch of pieces. I'm just one piece. The rest of the pieces are my teachers."

He did excel at one thing at Princess Anne High School: skateboarding. Indeed, he was given the nickname Skateboard P – and, he later winced, the occasional soubriquet "Oreo" for being (like the biscuits of the same name) black but, given his penchant for rock music and skate culture, "white" on the inside.

"The first sport I got into – and the one that has had most impact on my life – is skateboarding," he told the *Guardian* in 2008. "Most people think skateboarding is for some kid with blond hair from suburbia. But I remember when I was 12 or 13, growing up in Virginia Beach, everybody, black and white, was doing it. Skating taught me what it meant to be cool, to have credibility. I had it. I got so mad with it that I had a half-pipe [a structure used for skateboarding] put in my house. I had the look – the baggy jeans, the Vans. I still wear Vans shoes. I rap about skateboarding."

It was through the sport that he learned about "discipline and execution", essential qualities for a successful career in music.

He discovered music at a young age. In a discussion about music for *Interview* magazine in 2003 with Michael Jackson – one of his musical heroes – he revealed that he discovered The Isley Brothers, Donny Hathaway and Stevie Wonder through his father. "Those chord changes. They take you away," he said.

Music was both practical pursuit and listening pleasure. Music would be everywhere, indoors and out. "Music was so real to me, and so ubiquitous," he admitted to Oprah Winfrey in 2014. "It was in the air, everywhere we went."

His earliest musical memory is of wandering around amusement park Kings Dominion, and watching country star Kenny Rogers perform. As a child, he and his aunt used to sit in front of the stereo and play records back to back. One of the first albums he was moved to buy was by hip hop group A Tribe Called Quest. But it wasn't just black music that he was exposed to – he heard all sorts. "The radio station I listened to would play Queen, then Michael [Jackson], then Stevie [Wonder], then Genesis, then Madonna."

Growing up, Williams' musical influences were as diverse as the music he now makes. He listened to everyone from Michael Jackson and Stevie Wonder to Queen and Guns N' Roses. A particular favourite was the "dreamy, psychedelic" sound of The Isleys, he told eccentric Canadian celebrity interviewer John "Nardwuar" Ruskin. He told another reporter that he made a point of allowing himself to enjoy all types of music by not tying his identity to any one genre. "I love [hip hopper] Kool Moe Dee, but I also love [country-rock band] America," he said. "And I would never let my appreciation for one kind of music keep me from listening to another."

His Virginia neighbours inadvertently introduced him to seventies and eighties R&B as he rode his bike through the streets. From open windows he would hear blaring out the joyous funk, disco and soul of Luther Vandross, Earth, Wind & Fire and Chaka Khan. In fact, his senses were so enlivened by the music that he was overwhelmed. He even believed that he shares a condition with one of his heroes, Stevie Wonder, synaesthesia, which leads to the impression on the part of "sufferers" that, for example, you can smell colours or taste sounds.

"I see colours when I hear music – all sounds have a colour," he revealed to Oprah Winfrey. "When I hear a certain chord structure [by Wonder] I see mustards and yellows and browns.

But Stevie might hear it and go, 'What do you mean? Those are turquoise!'"

His belief that he had this condition perhaps enhanced his feeling of apartness from his fellow high school students. As he told Winfrey: "I didn't know why I was different, but I was different."

Music would prove his salvation, and confirmation that his difference had a purpose. At school, Williams would tap out rhythms on the classroom desks. His grandmother – with whom he spent a lot of time while his parents were working – soon noticed his musical potential and suggested he join the school band. He took her advice and decided to become a percussionist, joining the school marching band as drumline member (top bass) of the Fabulous Marching Cavaliers (FMC) of Princess Anne High School.

Williams' involvement in the school band provided two key tools for his adult success: the ability to read music, and punishing self-control. "Being a drummer is mega-macho," Williams told *People* magazine. "I'm constantly pushing myself. I got that from band camp. We were pushed on a military level."

The band used to play at local American football games and had as their tenor saxophonist (although some reports describe him as their conductor) a young man by the name of Chad Hugo, a student at the nearby Kempsville High School. Born in Korea, Hugo was the son of Filipino parents: a laboratory technician mother and retired Navy officer father. Like Missy Elliott, he was from the Portsmouth district and, also like her, was one of thousands of local youths in town because of the nearby Norfolk Naval Station. According to the *LA Times*, in an article assessing the impact of the station on the area's music scene, the diverse nature of the inhabitants from all over America there because of the military, and the consequent large number of young people, created a thriving, energetic and eclectic scene.

"This is a place where artists are free to experiment because you don't get pigeonholed," said Eric Spence, general manager of Beat Club Records, the label founded by Timbaland.

To Williams, it was a mainly characterless suburban district whose very ordinariness provided him with a blank canvas onto which he could project his imagination. "Ain't nothing spectacular about it," is how Timbaland described Virginia Beach to the *New York Times* in 2004. "Ain't nothing going on out there, really."

"We're from the suburbs," agreed Williams, "and the suburbs are pretty much the same everywhere you go, just like the projects are the same everywhere you go."

In Hugo's estimation, Virginia Beach is "sort of suburban-slash-melting-pot-slash-conservative. We're on the northernmost part of the Bible Belt."

Hugo and Williams initially met when they were in seventh grade, aged 12, during band class. It wasn't until a few years later, however, at a summer camp for gifted and talented, artistically inclined children, that Williams and Hugo became good friends and began to hang out.

It was the last in a series of fortunate incidents. His grandmother had referred him to his first music teacher, Mrs Warren, who then passed him on to her husband, Mr Warren, and then on to Mrs Edwards and Mr Sharps, music teachers at the camp. "Break one link in that chain," Williams has said, "and you might well have had a different story."

When Williams met Hugo: it was one of those lucky encounters, or re-encounters, that have seismic repercussions, like the one when Lennon met McCartney or Jagger met Richards.

"Pharrell was playing drums, and I was playing tenor saxophone," Hugo recalled. "Have you seen that movie, *School Of Rock*? That was us, except we played jazz standards like Herbie Hancock's 'Watermelon Man'."

Williams told CBS News that they soon began to spend a lot of time at each others' houses, particularly Hugo's, due to the high technology quotient there. "Pharrell and I would experiment recording with the two cassette decks that I had at my house," said Hugo, who has often belied his image as "the quiet one" by talking freely whenever he, and not Williams for a change, has been solicited for quotes about this stage in the pair's development.

"Like a lot of Filipino parents, mine had a piano in the house, hoping for their kids to learn how to play," he reminisced. "So that's what my brother and I did. We both took up sax, too. But I was doing it more for the fun of it. I'd learn how to play the songs on the radio. Pop culture has always been important to me, always knowing what was cool. I remember the first time I saw Herbie Hancock's 'Rockit' video [1983] and when Michael Jackson first did the moonwalk on the Motown awards."

Hugo remembers that first historic encounter with Williams as though it was yesterday.

"It was in band class. He was playing drums, and I could tell that he wanted to play hip hop beats," he said, his reminiscence including some criminal activity. "He was rapping, and I was into DJing and equipment. I had stolen a Casio SK-5 from a store, back when I was wearing a trench coat. We returned the drum machine back to the store after we started doing good in our careers! My parents wouldn't give me any money, always preaching about working your way up. I wasn't having it. A friend and I stole an Apple computer from the school library so we could start sequencing. Unfortunately, we got busted. I didn't care. I was going to do whatever I had to do to get on."

Williams recognised a kindred spirit in Hugo. "Most of us [at band camp] were kind of nerdy," he admitted in 2013. "Nobody walked in like Kurt Cobain or Dave Grohl-cool."

Williams and Hugo – who would later form the production duo The Neptunes – would make tracks "for fun", experimenting with samplers and beat production. Pharrell was the songwriter, while he and Hugo shared gadget duties. It was when they met another couple of local boys – Sheldon Haley, variously known as Shae or Shade, and Mike Etheridge – that they decided to form a band, one with which they could enter high school music contests. They, too, went by the name of The Neptunes, although somewhat confusingly it was a similar configuration, with Haley, Williams and Hugo, to the one that would later form the funk-rock band N★E★R★D.

"We wanted to show people what we were doing," Williams told a television reporter later in his career. "We didn't think, back in the mid-eighties, that it would end up here, with me talking about it on CBS News!"

Williams initially wanted to be a soul singer. "Yes, sir!" he told Ian Gittins of *Man About Town*. "That was the dream back then. But then I started writing songs, and producing them, and realised I could love that just as much."

At this stage, Williams never seriously believed that he would be able to make a living from music. "Not at all!" he said. "When I was growing up, doing something like this never seemed like a possibility. It wasn't on my wish list. I just figured I'd study my ass off and try to be some kind of art professor. But this happened instead and I am grateful."

When he was 18 years old, Williams actually had a couple of groups on the go: not just The Neptunes, the four-piece with Hugo, Haley and Etheridge, featuring Pharrell on drums and vocals, but also S.B.I., which stood for Surrounded By Idiots. S.B.I. was a short-lived hip hop venture with his friend Tim Mosley, then operating as Magnum DJ Timmy Tim, and rapper Melvin "Magoo" Barcliff, a friend from Norfolk, Virginia. "Tim was sick back then," Hugo said, which of course he meant as the highest praise. "He was doing Anita Baker and Michael Jackson loops."

"Going over to his house to make music was amazing," Pharrell exclaimed. "Timbaland is a genius. I still look up to him to this day."

It was believed that no S.B.I. tracks were ever recorded, but three from circa 1991 were later discovered. Using samples that would eventually provide the basis for other artists' hits, they were far more rhythmically and melodically sophisticated than might have been expected. There was 'Skull Caps & Stripe Shirts', which used a sample from Michael Jackson's 'Human Nature', ahead of later, similar usage by Teddy Riley for SWV's track 'Right Here' and Large Professor for Nas' 'It Ain't Hard To Tell'. Then there was 'If Ur Freaky Baby', based on another Jackson sample, this time from 'The Lady In My Life', as well as the hook from Lisa Stansfield's 'All Around The World', six years before Biggie Smalls employed it on Puff Daddy's 'Been Around The World'. Finally, there was 'It's Like That', which sampled Patrice Rushen's 'You Remind Me', well ahead of Junior M.A.F.I.A.'s 'I Need You Tonight'. One might not have been able to foretell worldwide fame and acclaim for Timbaland and Williams from these formative works, but they certainly showed some skills on their part.

"S.B.I. was a group that Timbaland had with Magoo that I was in," confirmed Pharrell in 2013. "At the same time I was with The Neptunes, who were then a group, a four-piece. I was in both scenarios. Tim's group was crazy."

Around this time, Pharrell had another "crazy" experience when he imbibed one too many hash cakes. "I fell asleep on the toilet after consuming six weed brownies," he told Nardwuar of his first dalliance with marijuana – he was always against smoking, and figured this was a safer way to ingest the narcotic, "so that it wouldn't affect my lungs". He remembers seeing and hearing things, before going to the bathroom and passing out.

"Very rarely," was his response to the enquiry, in 2014, as to whether he takes drugs. "I've had my share of pot brownies, but it's not my thing," he expanded. "I spend most of my time working." If anything, he admitted, he was a workaholic, and hard work required focus. "Lucidity is important to me," he said.

Not that he was always a goody-goody. As he explained to *Cosmopolitan* magazine, when he was 17 he got fired from McDonald's, on two counts: idleness, and theft. "I was fired from McDonald's because I was lazy," he confessed (he paid the company back karmically when, in 2003, he co-wrote and produced Justin Timberlake's 'I'm Lovin' It', which was then turned into a famous jingle). "Basically, I was getting in the way. After that, I worked at two other McDonald's, and they both fired me for the same thing.

"I never stole anything ever," he told MTV. "But I definitely kept a pocket full of chicken nuggets. They were so good... I got fired from three different [branches of the fast-food outlet]. I applied to a fourth but the other three jumped in and said: 'Listen, don't do it. He burns the meat and steals the chicken nuggets.'"

Mainly, though, Pharrell's adolescence appeared to have comprised lots of hard graft as he seized every opportunity to pursue a musical career. S.B.I. may not have led anywhere, but The Neptunes had better luck. Because one day in 1991, when Williams was 18, the band performed in a talent show at Princess Anne High School, and who should turn up but a talent scout sent by none other than that master of mechanoid future-funk – and producer of Michael Jackson and Whitney Houston, Bobby Brown and Usher – Teddy Riley, whose recording studio was a mere five-minute walk away.

It had been in the late eighties that Riley first considered a move out of his native New York. "I came down to Virginia Beach on a day trip with a bunch of my friends from Harlem," he explained. "We chartered two buses and came down for a picnic. I said, 'If I wanted to move anywhere, it would be here.' It's so calm, the atmosphere. So I moved my whole operation down here in 1990."

The move there was perfectly timed to coincide with the emergence of The Neptunes. And it was Riley who engineered their first meeting, even if, when he first encountered the future prime movers of avant-R&B, he assumed they were just a bunch of snot-nosed school-kids trying to gain access to his studio fortress.

"My first encounter with Pharrell was when they were trying to get to the studio because they thought my studio was just a studio you rent out," he said. "They didn't know that it was my studio and that it was private, so they tried to get in and I didn't let them in. I thought they were just a bunch of school-kids because they had book-bags and everything and they were just out in the parking lot spittin'," he told BBC Radio 1Xtra.

Unbeknownst to Williams, Riley had been in charge of the annual talent show at Princess Anne High School since his arrival in Virginia Beach. And although when it was the turn of The Neptunes (with Hugo as DJ, the keyboardist and saxophone player, Pharrell on drums and vocals and extra assistance from Etheridge and Haley) they appeared to be playing fairly formless music over which Williams beatboxed and did what Riley termed "gibberish rappin'", there was something unusual and appealing about it all – not least because the others in the show were just offering a predictable slew of karaoke covers of Luther Vandross or Whitney Houston tunes. So Riley overruled the other judges and crowned The Neptunes the winners.

"It was like R&B meets techno/new wave/hip hop," he marvelled. "It sounds the way they sound now."

Once that first contact had been made between the group and Riley's scout, they were officially invited into his Future Recording studios, located at 4338 Virginia Beach Avenue, after which The Neptunes were signed. At first, they signed to Riley as a band and they would work on their own music, until eventually he asked whether they had any songs to offer him.

"That's when Pharrell and I started working together as a production team, and that's also basically when we formed The Neptunes," confirmed Hugo. "We were about 17 or 18 years old. Right after we graduated from high school."

Even at this early stage in their development, the pair had fairly evenly divided roles, with Williams in charge of drum patterns, melodies for their beats and lyrics, and Hugo assisting with melody, enhancing the beats and arranging. Although the setup was nothing if not flexible.

"That's how we make our beats 80 percent of the time," Hugo explained. "But sometimes it varies according to the song. Sometimes we change roles and I write the chords and programme the drums. Pharrell is pretty good on sequencing as well. Sometimes he creates the basic sequence, then I add more sounds to it, or sample something to add to the sequence."

There was no looking back now for Williams, who took to his shiny new environs like a duck to water. An overly excitable duck. "Teddy's studio – that, wow, pretty much changed my life," he told Nardwuar, recalling the days when he and his team would work on tracks influenced variously by Depeche Mode and A Tribe Called Quest. "We were desperately just making music, taking those songs apart and seeing how they worked. We became a little group – Chad, Shay and our homeboy Mike Etheridge. That's what we would do after school every day. The studio was adjacent to our school. He [Riley] sent this guy over to see us, and the rest is history."

Or rather, hysteria. Because that was how Williams felt – besides himself with glee, barely able as he was to contain his pleasure at the technological palace that was Future Recordings. All he needed now was to brush up on what he called his "studio etiquette".

"My studio etiquette was so wrong," he laughed. "I'd be interrupting engineers and getting the dirtiest looks!"

He remembered one of the studio mixers/engineers, Jean-Marie Horvat, sitting him down and reminding the ebullient Williams who was in charge. "He would tell me, 'Teddy's the boss. You're lucky to be in the room. When he's working, just sit quiet and absorb everything that you can. And when you have the opportunity to ask him a question, do so. But you can't just call out. You need better studio etiquette. Teddy can see the talent in you, but you have to calm down.' Chad was quiet, he was cool, but I was hotheaded and fiery. I'd be, like, 'Change that chord! Change the snare!' And they'd be, like, 'Pipe down!'"

Riley was impressed by the core duo of Williams and Hugo, but he wasn't quite sure how to harness their talents. "I tried to keep them as busy as I could," he said. "I didn't have time to put out a record by them, but I didn't want to disappoint them. I gave them stipends, just to keep them motivated."

Nevertheless, he knew they were special: "architects", as he subsequently referred to them, of a whole new sound. He has since acknowledged their impact on music over the last two decades. The history of R&B, dance and pop – the world's most popular music – has been largely dominated by producers, he seems to recognise, from Motown's Holland-Dozier-Holland through Kenny Gamble and Leon Huff's Philadelphia Sound, onto the disco era's Nile Rodgers and Bernard Edwards of Chic and their eighties progeny Jimmy Jam and Terry Lewis. Jam and Lewis passed on the baton to New Jack Swing-era producers such as Riley and Kenneth "Babyface" Edmonds as the music became increasingly digitised, and they in turn handed it to Pharrell and his obvious peers, Timbaland, Dallas Austin and Rodney "Darkchild" Jerkins.

"Our music – Pharrell, Timbaland, myself, and producers like Rodney Jerkins – is before its time," Riley declared to Radio 1Xtra, going on to compare Williams, unexpectedly, to "the Head Martian". "We're different," he said. "We think differently."

The first example from Pharrell Williams of such different thinking to enter public consciousness came in 1992. According to Chad Hugo, Williams began by freestyling (rapping) in front of Riley; out of that came a section of 'Rump Shaker', a rap single by a New Jack Swing/hip hop troupe called Wreckx-N-Effect. The famous verse for the song, penned by a 19-year-old Pharrell, included the immortal line, "It's Teddy, ready with the 1-2 check-a, Wreckx-N-Effect is in effect but I'm the wreck-a!"

"That," said Hugo, "is when we started writing for Teddy."

Wreckx-N-Effect had formed in 1988 as the trio Wrecks-N-Effect, but after some success – and the death in a shooting of their member Brandon "DJ B-Dog" Mitchell – they shrank to a duo, comprising Aqil "A-Plus" Davidson and Teddy Riley's brother, Markell. Their second album, *Hard Or Smooth*, was a two million-selling US *Billboard* Top 10, and 'Rump Shaker' was its standout track, not to mention a glittering showcase for Riley's young protégé.

It was rumoured that Pharrell, along with fellow Neptune Chad Hugo, contributed additional production work to the song, but it was later confirmed that Riley and Tyrone "Ty" Fyffe alone produced it and that Williams' only contribution was in the lyric department.

Still, it was a stellar, supremely infectious, not to mention platinum-selling, start to Williams' career, even if, paradoxically, it was actually for his sonic, not lyrical, prowess that he would eventually make his name and earn his place in the history books. Based around a saxophone sample from the 1972 tune 'Darkest Light' by Lafayette Afro Rock Band and a drum sample from 'Midnight Theme' by Manzel (ironically, given that The Neptunes, and Pharrell, subsequently largely eschewed the use of samples), 'Rump Shaker' opened with Teddy Riley chanting the chorus, "All I wanna do is zooma-zoom-zoom-zoom in a poom-poom." Released in August 1992 – and propelled by a popular, if mildly controversial, video depicting Wreckx-N-Effect and Riley hosting a party at Virginia Beach, surrounded by legions of women in bikinis – it became one of the sounds of the summer, kept off the top slot only by Whitney Houston's version of Dolly Parton's 'I Will Always Love You'. It has subsequently become something of a popular culture staple, appearing in the background of a scene in the 2005 comedy film *The 40-Year-Old Virgin*, in episodes of TV series *Lost*, *Ugly Betty* and *My Name Is Earl*, even on the Xbox 360 Kinect video game *Dance Central*.

Williams' role in the track might have been reduced to a lyrical cameo, but he proved in his verse for Teddy Riley that he had a knack for a killer hook, one that would later manifest itself in the beats and melodies of The Neptunes' – and N.E.R.D.'s, and Williams' solo – work. It was lift-off time for Pharrell. And he was still in his teens.

"I was 18 in the music industry, and by the time I was 20 I was already looking out for my mom and dad," he once said, with his customary cool assurance. "Then, when I turned 24, so they would have no more worries, I bought them a house."

It was a house bought with the proceeds from early Neptunes productions, marking the start of a staggeringly successful run that would see the duo utterly dominate pop music at the turn of the century.

CHAPTER 2

Things Are Getting Better

"I told you that Pharrell was the new Quincy Jones. I sensed it in 1998"
— Noreaga

The clue lies in their name: N★E★R★D. The acronym of the digital rock band formed by Pharrell Williams and Chad Hugo, it stood for No One Ever Really Dies. The idea was that here was an antidote to rap braggadocio, offering hip hop for listeners who flaunted their difference, their outsider credentials. Because that's what Williams and Hugo were: avatars of a new R&B that couldn't be categorised as black or white, made by producer-writers-musicians who refused to be limited in any way, with more of a penchant for the cosmic than the worldly concerns of many of their peers.

Their other name — The Neptunes — was also key. Williams explained its provenance, and its appropriateness in their scheme of things. "The name just sounded right — Nep-tunes!" he beamed, admitting to Paul Elliott of Q magazine that he and Hugo were "infatuated with water. There's 85 per cent water in your body, and everything travels through your body through electric current. We were, like, cool – water is the best conductor in the world, so we'll be called The Neptunes. We'll be the kings of the water, like King Neptune.

"But that became too limiting because it was on planet Earth," he continued. "Then we realised if we named ourselves The Neptunes as in the planet Neptune, it's out of this world, and if it's out of this world, there's nothing we can't do in this world. That's what we're still trying to live up to."

It transpired that Williams – who once said, "I've always been a little bit left-of-centre" – was a huge fan of both the late US cosmologist Carl Sagan and of *Star Trek*; he even named his record label Star Trak in tribute.

"*Star Trek* is incredible because it reminds us that there is so much more out there!" he enthused to Ian Gittins of *Man About Town*. "Carl Sagan, who was a genius, said that our solar system – not our planet, but our solar system – is but one grain of sand on the beach of existence, and I truly believe that."

He also believed in alien life forms. "Well, think about it!" he urged. "Our solar system has nine planets, right, and it is just one of a trillion solar systems in the little sector of the boondocks of the Milky Way. One of a trillion! So even if we forget everything outside of that, that is nine trillion planets – and people really think we are the only life? The sheer numbers tell us that we can't be the only life form! The problem is there are these huge distances between the solar systems and no living species can make it that far unless they can harness the technology of wormholes."

Clearly, The Neptunes were a breed apart from the usual purveyors of hip hop or R&B. By all accounts, Williams didn't smoke and rarely drank alcohol, and in terms of dress he was likely to be seen in thrift-store polo shirts and a ragged trucker-style mesh baseball cap, with only a bling-y diamond-encrusted watch hinting at ghetto fabulous convention. Meanwhile, Hugo, one journalist noted, wore such everyday garb as cargo pants and a black T-shirt.

"When we were younger, we loved hip hop, but we were always looking for something alternative," Hugo reflected.

"Chad was a different cat, and he was cool with that," confirmed Williams.

"They weren't thugged-out beat boys from Harlem or Compton; they were band-camp nerds from Virginia Beach, Virginia," wrote Matt Diehl of the pair in *Esquire*. "In lieu of bragging about his dope rides, Pharrell waxed cosmic about blasting Stereolab [experimental electronic UK indie band] and Steely Dan in his pickup truck. They seemed like they were from another universe. In an era of hip hop artists wearing sagging waistlines and throwback jerseys down to the knees, Pharrell and Hugo walked into the room and their clothes actually, you know, fit."

As Simon Reynolds joked in his review of N★E★R★D.'s 2001 debut album, *In Search Of…*, while locating traces of sixties psychedelia and garage-rock in their music: "It's fair to surmise that these boys like the odd puff."

N★E★R★D may have been a quite different proposition to The Neptunes – they were, after all, a fully-functioning, live-performing rock band compared to the latter's studio unit – but they shared an ethereal-dreamer aesthetic. There was always something spacey, almost hippie-ish, about Williams. Like OutKast's André "3000" Benjamin, he was – still is – a hip hop kook. An article from around the time of Williams' emergence, by Kodwo Eshun, titled *N★E★R★D And The Rise Of New Geek Chic*, hailed a new archetype, the smart, witty, literate black nerd who, ignoring the playas and thugs, flaunted his love of sci-fi and white rock'n'roll. The video to N★E★R★D's 2004 single, 'She Wants To Move', referenced Queen's 'Bohemian Rhapsody'. And Williams was delighted to learn that the maudlin-rock band Coldplay included a version of a Neptunes production, Nelly's 'Hot In Herre', in their live set.

"Coldplay and Radiohead specifically I'd like to work with – Thom Yorke is dope," he once informed this writer.

Too popular to be picked on himself, nevertheless he was attuned, from an early age, to the plight of the weak. He explained to me why he wrote socially conscious songs that tenderly addressed the vulnerable and dispossessed. "We all encounter assholes in our lives that fuck with us," he said, alluding to Bobby James, a track on *In Search Of...*, about a teenager who is reduced to panhandling for dope money. Another mid-noughties N★E★R★D track, 'Thrasher', was, he said, "About a kid getting his ass beat and us just letting him know it's OK, you don't always win every battle in your life." He was, he insisted, a champion of the underdog. "One hundred per cent," he said, going on to describe his band as "backpackers in a world of drug-pushers".

Williams' black hippie consciousness, one that he and Hugo brought to bear on their productions with The Neptunes, meant eschewing rigid connections to any one genre or category. It also meant a certain flexibility when it came to musical ideas, a sonic openness and looseness, which is probably why it has been rare for any two Neptunes productions to sound the same even as they bear the instantly recognisable imprimatur of these two studio masters.

Pharrell's verse for Teddy Riley for Wreckx-n-Effect's 'Rump Shaker' became his entrée into the music industry, the starting shot for a marathon that continues to this day. His next job with Hugo was to remix 'Right Here', the debut single by US R&B trio SWV (Sisters With Voices). Featuring a much-used sample of

Michael Jackson's 'Human Nature' (from the album *Thriller*) and Williams rapping, "It's the S–the Double–the–U–the–V!!" over the music, it peaked at number two on the *Billboard* chart and number three in the UK.

Making further use of their Teddy Riley connection, The Neptunes next received co-writing and assistant production credits on Blackstreet's 1994 debut album, on the track (and sixth single from the album) 'Tonight's The Night', which also featured SWV (elsewhere, on the ballad 'Happy Home', Hugo played sax). Then, in 1996, they wrote and produced 'Use Your Heart', the second single from SWV's second album, *New Beginning*, which reached number six on the R&B/Hip Hop *Billboard* chart and number 22 in the main chart. They also contributed 'When This Feeling' to the same album. That year saw them, in a rare move, base another co-production and co-write for a US R&B girl trio on a sample – 'When Boy Meets Girl' by Total was propelled by a breathy, melodic section of The Bee Gees' 'Love You Inside Out' – although this may have been because it was a joint venture with Sean "Puffy" Combs, aka multimillionaire rap mogul Puff Daddy/P Diddy, who has never been averse to basing a rap track on an already well-known piece of music.

Then again, it could be argued that the first Neptunes production that sounded like The Neptunes was 'Lookin' At Me' by American rapper Mason Durell Betha alias Ma$e, which featured Puff Daddy. At once menacingly louche and breezily melodic, it was notable for its minimalist instrumentation and off-kilter synth line, one seemingly at odds with the bass and drums. The effective use of space was soon to become a Neptunes trademark. 'Lookin' At Me', featuring a snippet of Illegal Search by LL Cool J (later sampled by Kanye West for his 2012 single 'Cold', as was the Ma$e track itself), was an early example of Williams and Hugo's ability to combine the experimental with the commercial: the third single from Ma$e's 1997 debut album, *Harlem World*, it reached number eight in the States and went gold.

Another single that advanced The Neptunes' reputation and made them increasingly the go-to producers of the day was the 1998 track 'Superthug' by Victor Santiago Jr aka Noreaga, sometimes known as N.O.R.E., formerly one half of East Coast rap duo Capone-N-Noreaga. Instead of allowing his career to be derailed when Capone was sent to prison not long after the release of 1997's highly-regarded *The War Report* album, Noreaga went solo. The wisdom of his decision was evident from the opening bars of 'Superthug'.

There was so much to take in: Noreaga's bugged-out, manic rapped catchphrase "whut! whut! whut!" and the eerie, sung backing cries of "what? what? what?" variously attributed to R&B singer Tammy Lucas (an associate of Teddy Riley who had been on the panel of that high school talent show won by The Neptunes) and Neptunes protégée Kelis Rogers. Then there was the melodic allusion to Blondie's 1978 pop-disco classic 'Heart Of Glass' (Debbie Harry and Chris Stein, the song's composers, received a credit on 'Superthug'), not forgetting the jagged, buzzing synth pattern that reproduced the sound of an electric guitar, a dry run for its similar use on N★E★R★D's 2001 single, 'Lapdance'. 'Superthug' was an arresting production.

"The first time we heard this beat, it was truly one of those 'What the fuck is that?' moments in hip hop," wrote a contributor to the website Complex, which ranked it at number 28 in its list of the 100 Greatest Hip Hop Beats Of All Time. As with Ma$e's 'Lookin' At You', its radical sonics proved no barrier to commercial appeal: the second single from the Puerto Rican-American rapper's debut solo album, *N.O.R.E.*, it reached number 36 on the *Billboard* Hot 100 and top spot on the Hot Rap Tracks chart. It was also sampled by Janet Jackson for 'Ruff (I Like It)', recorded for her 2004 *Damita*

Jo album produced by The Neptunes, but oddly failed to make the cut. It certainly made the cut on MTV – for months it was the instrumental music of choice between videos.

'Superthug' was a bolt out of the blue, the sort that makes you wonder: where did that come from? "We get ideas from everyday life," said Chad Hugo. "Whether it be a sound we hear while walking around or a sound we hear from a record. But the most important thing is to have the, 'Okay, I'm gonna make a beat today' mind state when you enter the studio.

"We never think too deeply," he added. "We just start playing the metronome and record all kinds of patterns. While doing that we come up with a dope pattern. If you have an open mind to music genres, you can experiment with a lot of things in hip hop."

He detailed some of the equipment that they used for the recording of 'Superthug' and subsequent releases – a Korg 01/W for sequencing, an Ensoniq ASR-10 for the drums, sound modules such as the Roland 1080 or the 2080 – and claimed a preference for analogue synthesizers while stressing the importance of the digital realm. "These days you can make dope music with just a notebook computer," he admitted.

Focusing on 'Superthug', he explained that he and Williams had set out to create a new kind of hip hop rock, with the rhythmic invention of the former and sculpted noise of the latter.

"We were trying to blend hip hop with rock, but we didn't know how to play guitars, so we made that sound on the keyboard," Hugo declared, revealing that the electrifying synth-guitar sound that dominates the track had been achieved using a clavichord.

As for Noreaga, he acknowledged that he had taken a chance in enlisting The Neptunes for the track, before they had become the established force they would be by the early-noughties, when they worked with some of the most stellar names in the music business.

"It's surreal for me," he said in an interview with HipHopDX, discussing Williams' transition from anonymity to global ubiquity. "I look at it and I remember the times I was trying to bring Pharrell to certain artists, bring him to a Jay [Z] or bring him to a Nas or bring him to whoever was hot at the time. I remember those days and I remember people saying, 'Yo, I'm not sure about this kid.'"

Sceptics, he claimed, doubted Williams' abilities as a producer, whereas he believed he was "the hip hop Quincy Jones", a visionary soundscaper with a symphonic range. "When I get cocky," he said, "I feel like, 'I told you so, niggas. I told you so, the world. I told you so… I told you this, man. In 1998, I told you, man. I felt it. I knew it.' So I'm hands-down, astronomically so proud of that guy, man. I got to enjoy being there in the beginning. I get to witness what he's doing now. I still get to be there. I get to be the first person to say, 'I told you that Pharrell was the new Quincy Jones. I sensed it in 1998.' But nobody listens to N.O.R.E. because N.O.R.E.'s the thug dude that runs around, goes to parties and pops champagne and he's always drinking and having a good time. How could you believe that guy? But I told you in 1998. I seen it coming."

Williams' genius, said Noreaga, was his ability to tune into "thug music" even though, as Williams admitted, "I don't have a thug bone in my body." It is that chameleonic quality that has enabled him to create everything from edgy street anthems to upbeat party tunes such as 'Happy'. No wonder the biggest superstar of them all expressed an interest in using the 'Superthug' beat, as Noreaga discovered in a disarming phone call one night.

"Did I think he [Williams] was gonna be this huge?" Noreaga wondered aloud to HipHopDX. "Yeah, yeah, yeah. Yeah, I knew it. This dude called me and said Michael Jackson said he wanted 'Superthug'. Do you know how scary of a moment that was for me? Pharrell called me when 'Superthug' was out and said, 'Yo,

I sent Michael Jackson beats… A whole bunch of R&B beats.' So I'm sitting back, like, 'Okay. Why are you telling me this, Pharrell?' He says, 'Because Michael told me he don't want that. He wants 'Superthug'.'"

Asked whether he believed Williams should have more openly expressed his gratitude to him, either at the time or after he became acclaimed around the world, for taking that risk and hiring him as his producer back when he was a newcomer, Noreaga replied that the pleasure was in being present as he began his irresistible rise. "Pharrell, all he owes me is to be real with me," he said. "That's it. He doesn't owe me shit. I got a chance to witness him in the beginning and I enjoyed that."

'Superthug' made The Neptunes as sought after as the likes of Holland-Dozier-Holland and Gamble & Huff in their respective heydays. Before the end of the decade, they would work with MC Lyte, Brand Nubian, Noreaga again, The Wu-Tang Clan's infamous Ol' Dirty Bastard, even remixing Prince. But it was one commission in particular at the end of the century that opened the floodgates and made them not just the most in-demand producers in rap, but in pop per se.

It was their first venture to mark them out as auteurs, as producers capable of creating a coherent piece of work for a musician that effectively represented that performer while simultaneously reflecting their own artistic vision. *Kaleidoscope* – the debut solo album by singer, songwriter and sometime model Kelis Rogers – was the duo's first full album production. And even though it only fared moderately well in terms of sales, reaching number 144 on the *Billboard* 200 and number 43 in the UK, where it was eventually certified gold, as a statement of The Neptunes' abilities it was a resounding success with significant repercussions.

Recorded throughout 1998 and '99 at Master Sound Recording Studios, located in Virginia Beach, and released on December

7, 1999 by Virgin Records (with an early mention of Star Trak Entertainment, Hugo and Williams' label from 2001 onwards, in the sleeve credits), Kaleidoscope featured 14 tracks and over an hour of music, all of it written or co-written, produced, arranged and largely performed by Williams and Hugo. It was a tour de force of innovative sounds and production wizardry, the actual sonics taking centre stage with the subtle force of Kelis herself, which is saying something.

Kaleidoscope was most people's introduction to the 20-year-old Kelis Rogers, although she had already appeared on records by Wu-Tang Clan affiliates Gravediggaz, Pras, Ol' Dirty Bastard and Noreaga, as well as a Neptunes remix of Puff Daddy's *PE 2000*. The Amazonian warrior princess on the front cover with the shock of multicoloured hair and vividly painted face and body ("Everyone's so fixated on black and grey," she said at the time. "I'm not afraid of colour") heralded a musician with a strong visual sense. She had always been fascinated with fashion, and that fascination impacted on the artwork for the album, and on Williams. He later credited the fantastical creature with the dazzlingly hued hair and fierce demeanour with changing his own attitude towards style.

"I'd just signed this girl called Kelis, and back then all I wore was Ralph Lauren's Polo, because that was the thing," he said. "And Kelis turned to me and said, 'You've got to get out of this box.' She introduced me to Prada and Gucci. It was thanks to Kelis I discovered a life outside of monograms."

Looking like a cyber Tina Turner dipped in Day-Glo paint, she seemed to have beamed down from outer space or at least was preparing to go back there. "I fantasise about futuristic places that nobody's ever been to," declared the sci-fi-obsessed former drama student, who dreamed of assuming the role of superheroine witch-priestess Storm in the superhero franchise X-Men. "I don't feel restricted by boundaries because it's all in my head. You can't tell me I don't feel like it's the year 3000 because you haven't been there."

Apparently meditating or lost in silent prayer on the sleeve, she presented a singular, striking image. And yet her back-story was more earth-bound than her alien appearance suggested. She was born and raised in New York, with her three sisters, by religious, musical parents. "I remember being in the womb, my mom playing music to me. [And] my father was a musician. I grew up in Harlem, which is a real special place full of culture and music," she said.

Her father, who died around the time of *Kaleidoscope's* release after suffering a heart attack while scuba-diving, was an African-American Pentecostal minister, a former professor at Wesleyan University, and a part-time jazz saxophonist. Her half Chinese and half Puerto-Rican mother ("who had a sixth sense... definitely") was a fashion designer. Her parents came up with Kelis' unusual first name by fusing together their own: Kenneth and Eveliss.

Less harmonious were relations at home when Kelis was growing up, especially as she entered her teens. As a child, Kelis sang in church choirs and played violin, piano, and saxophone while attending Manhattan Country School, a private school. But when she turned 13 she shaved off all her hair, a sign of rebellions to come. Because of her parents' strong religious principles and her own free-spirited nature, there was inevitably conflict. Tensions were heightened by Kelis' loathing of school, which itself was exacerbated by her feelings of isolation brought on by her difference from the hordes.

"Kids are so obnoxious!" she complained. "It was a constant battle to belong. I'd say I live in this world, but I'm not of it. My mom always taught me, when I was little, to set myself aside from the bullshit."

It's not clear whether she left home at 16, or if she was kicked out by her mother at the same age. "I could've gone back if I'd humbled myself," she said later, "but that's not what I'm good at."

Still, the move worked, seeming to give her the push she needed to pursue music. Her packed CV included a lengthy apprenticeship in the Girls' Choir of Harlem, forming the R&B trio BLU (Black Ladies United), bartending, and working as a sales assistant in a clothing store. She also spent some time as a drama major at the Fiorello H. LaGuardia High School of Music & Art and Performing Arts, the one that inspired the 1980 movie (and 1982 TV series) *Fame*. It had a "nice vibe… academics are not my thing, y'know?" she said. Indeed, acting seemed to be the more obvious career path.

"I would still like to act, but I ended up stumbling into music," she once joked. "I was never that set on a singing career. I guess it was lucky that I wasn't tone deaf, huh?"

It was after college that a friend of a friend put her in touch with The Neptunes, a risky move for Kelis given that they were largely an unknown quantity – apparently, there was on the table an equivalent deal with The Wu-Tang Clan. Instead, she formed a bond with Williams and Hugo ("Chad is like my brother," she said in 2000. "He lets me do whatever I want") and negotiated her own record contract with Virgin.

Kaleidoscope was a collision of Kelis' audacious character and The Neptunes' bold production strokes. The title seemed to suit the music's rainbow alliance of sounds and styles, and its ever-changing nature. "It just seemed to fit," noted Kelis, recalling the childhood toy of the same name. "My mom used to buy kaleidoscopes for me as a kid, and later I started to think… the picture's never the same. It's reality, because it's what we see, but it's only a reflection."

The nineties saw a wave of new artists operating in the realm of R&B – one thinks of the so-called "neo soul" movement comprising the likes of D'Angelo, Maxwell, Lauryn Hill and Erykah Badu – but those artists came from a more conventional place than Kelis, Williams and Hugo. The only other relevant comparisons, in terms of the futuristic edge they brought to their work, were Missy Elliott, or Timbaland in tandem with Aaliyah: as with the latter, it seemed as though The Neptunes had found their muse, their lab pilot, on whom they would test their most radical beats.

Throughout, Kelis and The Neptunes evinced a determination to experiment and avoid cliché. It was a leap away from swingbeat with its unusual staccato rhythms and touches of otherworldly, Middle Eastern and Arabic influences.

The album opened with a two-minute prologue, during which Williams the cyber-narrator spoke wistfully of alien planets as though unveiling a sci-fi concept album and the listener got to hear Kelis grow from cute baby to sassy woman. 'Good Stuff' ("Telling you now, boy, put your eyes on me") was a stark, strident opening musical gambit, featuring Terrence "Terra" Thornton, otherwise known as Pusha T, a rapper from Virginia Beach who would soon figure large in The Neptunes' story as one half of hip hop duo Clipse. It also unveiled one of the album's leitmotifs – deceit – juxtaposing, "Said babe, I love you" with, "Yeah, he's lyin'..."

'Caught Out There' furthered the lyrical theme, and then some. It was the immediate standout, with its quintessential early-Neptunes attractions, all computer game bloops, electronic instrumentation, and the sort of arresting off-beat that was then en vogue in the productions of Timbaland and Rodney Jerkins. Over the music, Kelis – venting fury at her unfaithful lover – alternated between declaiming ("Yo, this song is for all the women out there who have been lied to by their men"), mellifluous singing, and yelling (after first cocking a gun), "I hate you so much right now!/ Arrrgghh!!! / I hate you so much right now!"

That yell was like several decades of feminism and riot grrrl rage compressed into one ferocious outburst. And it was effectively visualised by celebrated director Hype Williams in a video featuring the singer, all Technicolor blonde, gold, orange, red and fuchsia Afro, variously hospitalising her boyfriend, laying waste to his record collection, attacking her (male) shrink and galvanising an army of scorned placard-wielding females seeking vengeance on the faithless sex. At the end there was a brief glimpse of Pharrell, the first of many cameos in videos to come.

Ironically, given its status as a paean to female empowerment, 'Caught Out There' was, apparently, originally offered to rapper Busta Rhymes, who declined it. It was Kelis' gain. 'Caught Out There' was a show-stealer and calling card whose potency far outstripped its commercial achievements. Released as a single, it reached number 54 in the States, although it fared better across Europe, especially in the Netherlands and the UK, where it became her first Top Five hit, peaking at number three and number four, respectively. It enjoyed a cultural afterlife, too, cropping up on television whenever a programme required an injection of feisty venom. It also became common currency in relationships across the world and made Kelis the pin-up girl for irascibility and wrath.

"I'm hard to hide," she sighed, resigned to the fact. "I'm a homebody but once in a while I go out and I'm like, 'Oh my God!' I'll be having a conversation with my mom and people run up to me screaming, 'I hate you so much right now!' It's a little disturbing."

People would assume she was like that permanently, fixed in a state of man-loathing irritation. "Yeah, I get a lot of that – no big deal," she laughed. "Natural common sense tells you nobody can be one way all the time. But men come up to me and go, 'Hey, my girlfriend left that on my answering machine last night...' – and they love it."

She continued: "It's funny, I was living with someone for a few years so, er, a lot of things got attacked. Everyone gets angry, but I'm not afraid of my anger."

Not that the album was made in a state of high dudgeon. It was recorded, Kelis stressed, "with no negative thoughts or vibes going into it at all... That's very important." It was kaleidoscopic in terms of musical range and emotional tenor: she added that listeners were going to be disappointed, even shocked, if they imagined the record was all going to be, as she put it, "angry and mad".

It was far more diverse than that – The Neptunes, eclectic warriors of the recording studio, made sure of that. 'Get Along With You' was a new kind of R&B ballad or anti-love song, with an accompanying, appropriately goth-inspired video, although in its disavowal of materialism ("Don't need no beeper, don't need no cellular – I just wanna get along with you") it struck a conventionally romantic chord as a forlorn Kelis cooed over pizzicato strings and a strange quick-time beat. 'Mafia' continued the dark side of love theme as Kelis, to the strain of sitars, compared her feelings to those of the titular crime family.

"That's a metaphor for life and death and love, which are all the same thing, right?" she mused.

'Suspended' was something else again. "Don't wake me – I'm still dreaming," yawned Kelis over static, crackles and childlike synth twinkles. Throughout, shattering the lovely slow-motion tone and atmosphere of eerie dreaminess, a voice whispered, "Wake up, bitch!"

"That's what I call 'the reality demon'," explained Kelis. "Saying, 'Snap back from whatever state you're in.' There's always reality pulling you back from euphoria, but reality is the darker side."

'In The Morning' was a co-write between Kelis and The Neptunes, and featured Pharrell, in his familiar light, caressing tone, on the phone at the start wondering when Kelis, playing his long-distance lover, was leaving on a jet plane. 'Game Show' was quirky, playful, like a jazzy jingle for a futuristic kids' TV show. 'Ghetto Children', concerning domestic violence and self-love, was reminiscent of an old Stevie Wonder album track and featured R&B singer Marc Dorsey (the crooning veteran of at least three Spike Lee soundtracks: *Crooklyn*, *Clockers* and *Get On The Bus*). There was also a credit on the sleeve for N★E★R★D on instruments. 'Mars' had a virtually unquantifiable metre, and opened with Pharrell warning, "I think we have a problem." It was a metaphor about relationships, and loneliness.

"See, when I sing about Mars, I'm singing about not being alone," clarified Kelis. "I realise we're all alone here, but beyond that, it's about finding someone who's as alone, and able to relate to you on that level. Having a connection with them, and finding power and strength through each other." 'No Turning Back' had a jittery pulse reminiscent of Ma$e's 'Lookin' At Me', and some Pharrell ad-libs. 'Roller Rink' and 'I Want Your Love' rounded off a sterling first effort from Kelis and The Neptunes, one that set the standard for experimental R&B as the new decade dawned. Apart from the closing track, 'Wouldn't You Agree', which appeared to have strayed in from a far more conservative release, *Kaleidoscope* was an index of rhythmic and melodic possibilities.

"*Kaleidoscope* was more than I could have ever asked for," said Kelis. "It launched my career but also more than anything it solidified me as an artist, not as a singer, not as a pop star."

It established Kelis as an exciting new artist with a characterful vision who sang with a weary ennui seemingly beyond her years. More than that, it posited Williams and Hugo as the only serious contenders for Missy Elliott and Timbaland's future/avant-R&B

crown. Their blend of live musicianship (they played everything themselves) with sparse beats and a skewed sense of melody offered a new direction for soul and R&B.

Kaleidoscope's startling qualities were widely hailed by the press. *Uncut* magazine described it as an "elastic extravaganza" of hip hop, pop and R&B. "As hip hop stalls and 'soul' sinks ever further into sterile self-parody, this, with sublime arrogance, seizes the reins and makes a decision," wrote Chris Roberts. The album, he added, "has prompted the steamiest word-of-mouth since Macy Gray", adding: "*Kaleidoscope* is street-smart but ghetto fabulous. It could prove the biggest breakthrough since The Fugees' now-devalued *The Score*." *NME* was equally enraptured. "Uplifting, magical, genre-bending music. If there's a better debut album this year, bring it on. We need more like this," wrote the music weekly, which decided the Neptunes-Kelis collaboration "rewrote the rulebook of R&B". *Pop Matters* went further, crediting the album with tapping into a radical zeitgeist, placing 'Caught Out There' in particular in a lineage of black rage that included Nina Simone, Sly Stone, Miles Davis and Public Enemy, and praising it for restoring the balance in a "black masculine universe".

Furthermore, as a result of *Kaleidoscope*, Kelis won the BRIT Award for International Breakthrough Act and the *NME* Award for Best R&B/Soul Act in 2001, even if she was keen to distance herself from any generic pigeonholing.

"I was never an R&B artist," she insisted. "People coined me one but that's because, especially if you're in the States, if you're black and you sing, then you're R&B."

The album sold just over 281,000 copies in the US but fared better, comparatively speaking, in Britain, where it shifted 100,000 units and all three singles – 'Caught Out There', 'Good Stuff' and 'Get Along With You' – were hits (they also became mainstays on the likes of MTV, the Box and VH1). *Kaleidoscope* charted in numerous countries, including New Zealand, Sweden and Germany, and earned Kelis an international fanbase that she would cultivate through future releases and touring.

It also inspired a new generation of free-spirited, experimentally minded artists – R&B or otherwise – to use the music as a launchpad for their idiosyncratic visions. It could reasonably be argued that Kelis' team-up with The Neptunes paved the way for a musician of the singular calibre of Janelle Monáe, to name but one. *Kaleidoscope* expanded the remit of R&B.

And Pharrell had barely begun.

CHAPTER 3

Right For Me

"I was really inspired by The Neptunes. I just love their tracks. I wanted to make it a little bit nastier and funkier"

— Britney Spears

Already by 2001 the number of collaborators on Pharrell Williams' CV was well into triple figures. Indeed, he was so prolific in the wake of *Kaleidoscope*, it would probably be simpler to list the people he *didn't* work with. Over the ensuing few years he would produce some of the biggest acts on the planet, and have some of the biggest hits on the charts. He and Chad Hugo worked with R&B and soul musicians, boy bands and rock bands, hip hoppers and pop stars. Such was The Neptunes' midas touch, so all-encompassing was their remit, that the usual response when you mention a song or a performer that they produced during this period is, "What? *That was them as well?*"

Pharrell's work in the early-to-mid-noughties can be divided into five categories: his cameo appearances on other people's songs (that he also produced); his and Hugo's productions for multifarious artists as The Neptunes; their remixes of various tracks; his solo work; and his output with Chad Hugo and Sheldon "Shay" Haley as N★E★R★D. Hence that oft-repeated statistic, taken from a survey in August 2003, that found Pharrell and Co were responsible for almost 20 percent of songs played on British radio at the time, while a similar survey in the US was an even more impressive 43 percent.

According to Wikipedia in 2015, Pharrell's discography comprised two studio albums, two EPs, one mix-tape, 46 singles (including 38 as a featured artist) and 39 guest appearances. This seemed conservative to say the least. In 2000 alone, just some of the artists eager for Pharrell to sprinkle his magic dust on their music included Angie Stone, Backstreet Boys, Beenie Man, Ben Harper, Cole, Jay-Z, Lil' Kim, Ludacris, Mystikal, Rage Against The Machine and Sade. By 2001, an exponential growth in The Neptunes' reputation meant their ubiquity became total music business omnipresence: All Saints, Babyface, Basement Jaxx, Britney Spears, Busta Rhymes, Clipse, Daft Punk, Dr Dre, Foxy Brown, Garbage, Ice Cube, Janet Jackson, Limp Bizkit, Mary J Blige, ★NSync, No Doubt, P Diddy, Perry Farrell and Usher were some of those who solicited the input of Williams and Hugo that year.

But what was it about this softly spoken Virginian that led the great and the good, from hard-bitten veterans to mega-powerful newcomers, to seek out his studio alchemy? What was it that he brought to recording sessions?

"What I'm good at doing is holding up a mirror at an artist and showing them some of the things they've been ignoring about themselves," he revealed. "I can point things out: 'Hey, you know this is there, you have this, and maybe you should turn this up.'

"When I am producing with The Neptunes, I have no ego," he continued. "I let that go. I say to the artist, whether it be Beyoncé or Usher, 'What do you want to do?' And when they tell me, I say, 'OK, let's do it like this.' It's real simple."

It has been suggested that it is his diffidence that makes all the difference. His is the triumph of the beatific and calm. By taking a cool back seat he has allowed his various collaborators to flourish. He has given them the space to create. "I love to direct, to collaborate," he has said.

Speaking to *Time* magazine, Pharrell explained that "taking somebody from A to B is cool, but when we produce we want to take people from A to D, to challenge their artistic natures, their image, everything."

There was an exploration of The Neptunes' modus operandi in *Sound On Sound*, in an interview with Andrew Coleman, recording engineer for the duo at various studios in Los Angeles, New York, Miami and their home base of Virginia Beach. Coleman listed some of the equipment used in recordings – a master keyboard here and Korg and Roland sound modules there – but insisted that the mechanics of it all never overwhelmed the creative process.

"Pharrell is amazing," he said. "He has a vision for where each of the artists is going. He adapts to them, not the other way around. The artists aren't going into the same mould and coming out sounding the same at the other end." He added that Williams and Hugo "complement each other perfectly" and attempted to explain who did what.

"Pharrell is pretty much behind the keyboards or doing vocals while I keep the technical end running," he said. "He's incredibly creative and he expects things to be able to happen when he wants them to, that moment. He doesn't want to have to think about the technical part, and I will travel to where the artist is, get the songs written and do the tracks and the reference mixes. Chad will usually stay in Virginia Beach and handle all the mixes as they come in, putting other touches on."

He joked that it was rare to see Hugo and Williams in the same place at the same time.

"Sometimes you wonder if they're the same person," he laughed. "But no one person could do that much work."

Notwithstanding his ubiquity, Williams emphasised his anonymity. He stressed this point in 2014 in a conversation with Oprah Winfrey, during which she proclaimed it The Year Of Pharrell. Williams was as surprised as she was by his worldwide success. "Because," as he smiled, "you know me: I'm the guy standing next to the guy."

And then he expanded on the point to legendary radio presenter Howard Stern, also in 2014, explaining how he became first and foremost a behind-scenes technician rather than an out-front performer. Because it could so easily have gone the other way. "I wanted to be an artist in my twenties, in the very beginning," he said, revealing that it was actually his peers in the music industry who discouraged him from pursuing the idea of himself as the centre of attention. "But that was crushed by a bunch of 'no, no, no's' – 'you're weird, and you wear weird things. We'll just stick to the things that you write and produce for other people.' And I kind of got accustomed to that and started to enjoy writing through people and producing for people. Because I found people to have these really interesting, foreign energies that would inspire me and take me to places I wouldn't go on my own."

One of those interesting, foreign energies was Michael Lawrence Tyler, otherwise known as Mystikal, a rapper from New Orleans. Pharrell had already worked (in tandem with, not Chad Hugo, but New Orleans rap producer Leroy 'Precise' Edwards) with Mystikal, back in 1995, on a track from his debut album, *Mind Of Mystikal,* titled 'Not That Nigga', featuring Michelle Tyler. He and Williams had obviously clicked because, five years later, they were together in the studio again.

In July 2000, Mystikal released 'Shake Ya Ass', also known by its more daytime radio-friendly title, 'Shake It Fast'. It was the second single from his fourth album, *Let's Get Ready*, and was produced by both Neptunes. It also featured vocals from Pharrell Williams which, although uncredited, were surely a key to the song's success.

If the production found The Neptunes at their most playful – quirky, infectious, audaciously spacious – Williams' role was as the straight man to the comically priapic Mystikal ("I came here with my dick in my hand/Don't make me leave here with my foot in yo' ass"). Really, the single was as much of a showcase for Pharrell as it was for Mystikal; it saw the public unveiling of his airy, effortless Curtis Mayfield-esque falsetto. He dispatched with utter insouciance his chorus, treating the "playas" and "pimps" in the lyric as though they were characters in a nursery rhyme. But his voice was sufficiently light, breezy and anonymous that you could imagine it being employed in a variety of musical environments – which, of course, is exactly what did happen over the next few years. Pharrell's airy tone was the sublime counterpoint to Mystikal's ridiculous gruff rasp.

Whatever, the combination worked: the single was a huge success for both parties, peaking at number 13 on the *Billboard* Hot 100, number three on the Hot R&B/Hip Hop Singles & Tracks and number seven on the Hot Rap Singles. Speaking to language-decoding website RapGenius, Mystikal confessed to having doubts about the single at the start, wondering whether it should have been issued at all, so worried was he that it misrepresented him as a serious artist. In the end, he admitted, he was glad he changed his mind, especially when it became the "biggest song of my career". It also proved immensely adaptable to a whole variety of television and movie contexts, featuring in everything from *Kiss Of The Dragon* and *About A Boy* to TV series *Everybody Hates Chris* and the 2008 video game *Grand Theft Auto IV* during a strip club scene. The BMI (Broadcast Music, Inc, one of America's three performing rights organisations) may well have been scrutinising that scene, because it scored Williams a Songwriter Of The Year award.

The adaptability of The Neptunes continued apace as they gained their first worldwide hit in 2001 after teaming up with a quite different artist to Mystikal: teen pop sensation Britney Spears.

With her first two albums – ...*Baby One More Time* (1999) and *Oops!... I Did It Again* (2000) – Britney established herself as one of the biggest names in pop. But by album three, the 19-year-old was looking for a way to assert herself as an adult and as a more credible artiste. She did so with *Britney*, a 12-track collection that featured five Spears co-writes, as well as collaborations with some of the biggest, and most adventurous, names in R&B, including Rodney "Darkchild" Jerkins and, inevitably, The Neptunes (she also recorded songs with Missy Elliott and Timbaland, but their tracks never made the final LP due to "scheduling conflicts").

The idea, she said in an interview at the time, was to achieve an edgier, more urban and mature sound.

"This album I've been really inspired by a lot of hip hop and R&B, so when I went to this record, before I was even recording it, I was going to clubs and stuff. And the music that was really standing out for me was The Neptunes," she recalled. "Every time a song came on by them I was just like, 'Man, I have got to get up and dance.' So, you know, *NSync had worked with them and I told Jive [her label] that I think I really want to work with them.

"I don't think I'll ever be hardcore R&B," she mused. "I don't know who knows what I'll be like tomorrow, but for this album I was really inspired by The Neptunes. I just love their tracks. I definitely wanted to incorporate a little bit into it just to make it a little bit nastier and funkier."

She said that Williams and Hugo were "the funniest guys in the whole world to work with" in the studio. She explained that they initially recorded a ballad, "a beautiful folk song that didn't make the album", adding that "it'll probably go on the next album", although there was no such Neptunes acoustic ditty on 2003's *In The Zone*. She added that "we just hit it off and the music that they do for me is just kind of where I'm at right now. It really suits me and who I am." That, she insisted, was why the first single from Britney was 'I'm A Slave 4 U' – "because the song just really stood out, and it just kind of worked".

As an attempt to shake off her girl-next-door image, 'I'm A Slave 4 U' was perfect. It may have been written by Williams and Hugo, two men in their late twenties, but its message rang true for a young woman still in her teens. "I know I may be young, but I've got feelings, too. And I need to do what I feel like doing. So let me go and just listen," Britney breathily whispered at the outset, ahead of a (sung) couplet that neatly captured her desire for transition: "All you people look at me like I'm a little girl/Well, did you ever think it be okay for me to step into this world?" She proceeded to sing a lyric that read like an update of Madonna's 'Into The Groove' message of liberation via the dance floor.

After reading the lyrics for the first time, Spears commented that they were "about me just wanting to go out and forget who I am and dance and have a good time. That's kinda where I am right now. I love working, but at the same time, I love having a good time."

Recorded at Master Sound Studios in Virginia Beach, Virginia, with final production at Right Track Studios in New York, 'I'm A Slave 4 U' bore urban influences, Middle Eastern flavours, a minimalist atmosphere and the sort of textures and effects normally found in experimental electronica. There were hooks both musical and lyrical – the chorus, with its attendant "Get it get it, get it get it," which sounded like "Kitty kitty, kitty kitty", was immensely engaging – on a record that accomplished what it set out to achieve: make Britney seem as cutting edge as she was cute and coquettish.

The overall sound of the record was compared at the time to the 1982 song 'Nasty Girl' by Prince protégées Vanity 6 (which was also written by Prince), and there was a Prince-ish influence discernible – the "4U" of the title was certainly the sort of thing Prince would come up with – but sonically this was Prince fast-forwarded into a futuristic realm that he himself hadn't inhabited for years.

Apparently, Williams wrote 'I'm A Slave 4 U', and gave it to Spears after he was approached by Spears' then boyfriend. "Justin [Timberlake] made that introduction," Pharrell told Howard Stern. "She was open to it."

Stern marvelled at Williams' career, and the freedoms it afforded him, to be able to collaborate with whoever took his fancy at any given moment. It must be almost like, he said, forming a new group every time. "Like, you could go to someone like Britney Spears and say, 'Hey, I've got a great idea for you.' And then you come up with this ['I'm A Slave 4 You']..."

And yet, as it transpired, 'I'm A Slave 4 U' was originally written not for Spears, but for Janet Jackson, for her 2001 album, *All For You*. Why, wondered Stern, did she not record it? Surely, in the light of its global success, she must have kicked herself? Did she call up Pharrell and declare, "Shit, I should have done it!"

"That stuff rarely happens," laughed Williams. "Probably the only person that does that is Jay [Z]. He'll say, 'Pfft, I missed that one!'

"I don't know," Williams reflected further. "She [Jackson] was just in a different space at that time and I understood that it didn't make sense for her."

Did that, wondered Stern, make Williams even more determined to find someone who would transform the turned-down song into a big hit, so that the person who refused it would, in his words, "eat their hearts out"? "That," countered Williams, "has never been my motivation. There's a competitive thing where you want to be better, but that [sort of thing] is for the gym."

Spears premiered the song at the Metropolitan Opera House in New York City for the MTV Video Music Awards, on September 6, 2001, during which performance she wore a live albino Burmese python on her shoulders in a set designed to resemble a jungle, complete with a caged white tiger: it drew criticism from animal rights group PETA. In terms of commotion, it was a slight advance on her performance at the VMAs the previous year, when she removed most of her clothes during a rendition of The Rolling Stones' 'Satisfaction'. In August 2008, MTV named her 'Slave 4 U' performance the most memorable moment in VMA history.

An artist with a strong visual sense and an eye for outrage, Spears' video for 'I'm A Slave 4 U' – directed by Francis Lawrence, who had worked on videos for Aerosmith, Janet Jackson and Destiny's Child – featured the singer hoofing and generally sweating up a storm in a sauna. Ironically, given the song's pre-history, Spears' main influence in her performance of the song was deemed to be Janet Jackson. The video was ranked at number one in the list of the 50 Sexiest Music Videos of All-Time published by Canadian music channel MuchMusic in 2007.

Although the single, released in September 2001, only reached number 27 in America, it did become The Neptunes' passport to the world's charts, peaking inside the Top 10 in almost every country that it charted in, including number four in the UK. Critically, it got a mixed reception, some journalists praising Britney's new, grown-up direction, others unhappy with the synthetic, "unnatural" sound. *NME* called it "funk the way God intended – hypnotic, insistent, mysterious, suggestive". About.com hailed the "radical shift from the 'not quite innocent' 16-year-old schoolgirl of Britney's first album. Slinky and sexy have crept into the Britney Spears style." All Pop, on the other hand, complained that it was a "huge step away from the bouncy pop that made her a superstar", stating that 'I'm A Slave 4 U' "did not suit her style, the vocals were forced and the Janet Jackson slinkiness was unnatural".

Still, Britney herself was sure of her new direction. "I definitely think this is a turning point in my career," she decided. "I think that I'm really just coming into my own and becoming the person I want to be." And The Neptunes were helping her achieve this successful transformation, one that she continued with 'Boys', the other team-up on third album, *Britney*, with Williams and Hugo. A slower version of the album track, featuring Pharrell duetting with Britney, entitled 'The Co-Ed Remix', would be the sixth and final single from the *Britney* album when it was released in July 2002 (it would also be the second track lifted from the soundtrack of *Austin Powers In Goldmember*, following on from 'Work It Out', performed by one of the movie's stars, Beyoncé Knowles).

'Boys' was another song rejected by Janet Jackson, who essayed a demo of it before it was recorded by Spears. It met with a mixed commercial and critical response. It didn't fare spectacularly well in the States, where it was her least successful single to date, but it went Top 10 in the UK and Belgium and was later certified Gold in Australia. When AOL Music premiered the track, it was streamed more than 1.35 million times, setting a new record. *The Milwaukee*

Journal Sentinel proclaimed it a "rap-lite teen-pop tease" while David Browne of *Entertainment Weekly* dismissed it as a "cut-rate eighties Janet Jackson", adding that The Neptunes "swaddle her in writhing, kick-the-can beats, but never have a groove and a verse been so betrayed by a limp chorus". Others enjoyed the chemistry between Britney and Pharrell, and applauded the attempt by the producers to advance the shift by the artist from adolescence to adulthood: *Yale Daily News* writer Catherine Halaby considered the song "an envelope-pushing – when you consider her claims of wholesomeness – smutfest". Alex Needham of *NME* decreed it "a decidedly lubricious duet – she sings about boys, he sings about girls. A simple concept, but an effective one, resulting in Britney's best single [in] ages."

While they were producing the great and the good of pop, rock, soul and R&B, it made sense that The Neptunes would eventually hook up with Britney's sometime boyfriend, Justin Timberlake. This they did during 2002, when they worked with the *NSync boy band sensation on his debut solo album, *Justified*. Released by Jive (also Spears' label), it was written and recorded in a six-week period, during a hiatus from Timberlake's day job. As with Britney's third album, the intention was to present a more mature recording artist – the 21 year old received a co-writing credit on each of the 13 tracks. And as with Britney, he and his record label made the judgement that the swiftest route to maturity was the urban route: The Neptunes co-wrote and produced seven of the songs, with four offerings from Timbaland and additional contributions from hip hop/ R&B producers Brian McKnight, Scott Storch and Harvey Mason. Rap duo Clipse also made a guest appearance on one of the tracks, as did Janet Jackson.

The speed of the sessions – at Westlake Recording Studios in Los Angeles, Manhattan Center Studios in New York and Master

Sound Recording Studios and Windmark Recording in Virginia Beach – Chad Hugo attributed to Timberlake's work ethic.

"He's a really hard worker," he said. "He would stay up late every night just to finish up backing vocals. I think people want to put him in a box, a boy band box, or an *NSync box, but he's not like that. He's a real individual and a dope vocalist."

Timberlake put it down to a "creative spurt" reminiscent of "that period of time back in the sixties and seventies when musicians got together and just jammed and worked out of inspiration. There was no heavy calculation or belabouring songs and mixes. Everything flowed pretty easily and naturally," he told *Billboard*.

Timberlake told the magazine that he was amused by the media's insistence he'd been blatantly copping vocal licks from Michael Jackson on the first single from the album, *Like I Love You*, because he had actually been delving rather further back for inspiration: to seventies soul legends such as Donny Hathaway, Stevie Wonder, and Al Green.

"They're the artists who have shaped the way I approach music," he affirmed. "When I sing, I don't close my eyes and try to channel Michael Jackson, who has had an undeniable influence on me as a stage performer."

He singled out Hathaway, the troubled cult soul artist who took his own life in 1979. "I think about how 100 percent present he was in his songs," he said. "He seemed to be living each word, each syllable as he sang it. That's the energy I'm reaching for when I sing."

Despite the presence behind the recording console of the likes of Timbaland and The Neptunes – who in 2001 produced *NSync's Top 10 hit 'Girlfriend', from their album *Celebrity* – the young heartthrob insisted that he hadn't deliberately set out to make a "non-*NSync record" with *Justified*.

"I was just trying to make a multi-dimensional record," he explained, "a record that captured the vibe of my favourite time in music, the sixties. For the six weeks that we worked on these songs, I got to live in my own musical dream world and play a little hip hop, a little old-school R&B, a little classic rock. It was so much fun – and I learned a lot about making music in a totally different way than I was used to."

As far as The Neptunes were concerned, inspiration for the making of *Justified* came from a period a little after the sixties – the late-seventies symphonic boogie of Earth, Wind & Fire. Pharrell told MTV News that he, Hugo and Timberlake would drive around in his car listening to the orchestral disco behemoths' albums such as *All 'N All*, *Gratitude* and *I Am*.

"I was raised on Earth, Wind & Fire," Williams later informed the *Guardian*. "'Can't Hide Love' [from *Gratitude*] was the first record that influenced my life. My mom and dad used to play this song a lot when I was a kid. That song changed me. I think that's what made me a singer. In fact, Earth, Wind & Fire are probably what made me, full-stop – that's baby-making music, man!"

Unlike Timberlake, Williams did acknowledge the influence on *Justified* of Michael Jackson, revealing that he and Hugo listened to both *Off The Wall* (1979) and *Thriller* (1982) in the run-up to recording. "I remember watching [Jackson 5] on television when I was really young," Pharrell said. "The *Thriller* album also changed my life. 'Billie Jean' changed my life."

The plan on *Justified* was to create music that was similar to Jackson's work without "recycling it". Hugo commented that their intention was to re-create "that sense of those timeless, classic songs", without any of what he somewhat mystifyingly called the "'bling, bling, hit me on my two-way' style of the new R&B". *Justified,* Hugo decided, had "elements of the old and the new".

Ironically, after Janet Jackson passed on Neptunes material, it transpired that Michael Jackson had been first in the frame for the *Justified* demos, but he, like his sister, concluded that they weren't quite for him. Perhaps because he was just finished with the recording of his first album of new material in a decade, 2001's *Invincible*, his management rejected the eight songs offered by The Neptunes that would eventually form the bulk of *Justified*.

"Some of the songs were offered to Michael Jackson first," admitted Pharrell. "But Jackson's manager said the songs were not good enough so they were given to Justin Timberlake instead."

In his judgement, it was also because Jackson "heard too much of himself in them and thought they weren't challenging enough," he told Howard Stern, who was himself disappointed at Jackson's decision, the broadcaster proclaiming *Justified* to be "fucking killer". There was a third possible reason for Jackson's rejection of songs that had apparently been tailor-made for him: that he was looking for "edgier" material than the smooth, polished yet typically tricksy and intricately rhythmic tracks The Neptunes had prepared for *Justified*; something more along the lines of their work with rapper Noreaga.

"I'll never forget Michael's manager saying, 'Yo, Michael wants some 'Superthug'!," recalled Williams. "And I was like, 'What?' I remember being so baffled and so crushed, cos he still is my idol. It was definitely a bummer."

Williams actually got to meet his idol in June 2003, for an interview with the star that appeared in *Interview* magazine. In it, in an unexpected reversal of roles, Jackson played the part of the interrogator, Williams the interviewee. Although the "encounter" took place over the phone, Pharrell described it as "super-surreal". It began with the superstar asking the then-still-rising songwriter/ producer what inspired him, and he replied: "You treat the air as a canvas and the paint is the chords that come through your fingers, out of the keyboard. So when I'm playing, I'm sort of painting a feeling in the air." Jackson proceeded to elicit Pharrell's thoughts on new music and the direction his own music was taking. He answered that he was less influenced by upcoming artists that he was by the catalogues of Stevie Wonder, Donny Hathaway and Jackson himself.

"I'm taking notes from people like yourself, like not being afraid to listen to your feelings and turn your aspirations and ambitions into material. Making it happen, making it materialise," he said from his home in Virginia Beach. Williams then attempted to change tack, towards a discussion of Jackson's notorious public image, the rumours that surrounded his private life, and his resultant hounding by the media.

"People bother you," he ventured, "because they love you. That's the only reason why. When you do something that people don't necessarily understand, they're going to make it into a bigger problem than they would for anybody else because you're one of the most amazing talents that's ever lived. You've accomplished and achieved more in this century than most any other men.

"What you do is so amazing," he continued with his worship. "People are having children to your songs. You've affected the world."

"Thank you very much – it's like the bigger the star, the bigger the target," responded Jackson, who proceeded to make cautious comparisons between himself and a certain biblical deity. "I'm not being a braggadocio or anything like that, but you know you're on top when they start throwing arrows at you. Even Jesus was crucified. People who bring light to the world, from Mahatma Gandhi to Martin Luther King to Jesus Christ, even myself. And my motto has been Heal the World, We are the World, Earth Song, Save Our Children, Help Our Planet. And people want to persecute me for it, but it never hurts… I'm resilient. I have rhinoceros skin. Nothing can hurt me. Nothing."

Williams concluded the interview by saying, "I hope that I can be half as dope as you one day," adding: "If I never work with you, just know that you are unstoppable."

Williams and Jackson – who died, of course, in 2009 – never did get to work together, but the interview did grant him some insight into his hero's mind. And he did get to meet him in person eventually, a few years later, when he was invited to his Neverland ranch. This, too, Williams found a surreal experience, joined as he was by comedian Chris Tucker and the director of the *Rush Hour* movies, Brett Ratner, as well as some of Jackson's scarier animal pals.

"We were all riding around on golf karts that look more like sports cars at a time when I'd never seen anything like that before," recalled Williams. "And he had this carnival thing in his back yard and these big tiger cages: one big one named Simba and another called Thriller. And Chris Tucker's going, 'Let's go and visit the tigers!'"

Before that strange day, just after Williams and Hugo had modified the demos that Jackson had rejected and work had begun on *Justified* with Timberlake, Pharrell received a call from the ill-fated entertainer. With a mouth full of popcorn, he expressed surprise that The Neptunes had given the songs to the *NSync star, and, seemingly full of regret, took to singing the songs down the phone, word for word, note for note, "in Justin's style".

"It was then," Pharrell told the *Huffington Post*, "that I recognised the genius of the guy. He didn't miss a thing. Michael was one of the most incredible performers of all time. I'll never forget the day that he sang me those songs, sounding like Justin. And he said, 'You should've gave those songs to me.'"

Still, as Pharrell noted, there was a positive outcome to it all: *Justified*, the first great Justin Timberlake album and another superb example of The Neptunes' capabilities as studio auteurs (Timberlake alluded to the significance of their role on the inner sleeve of the album, where he thanked Williams, saying, "You were essential in making this album", and called Hugo, "My favourite Filipino").

Pharrell played down the fact that Jackson had chosen not to get involved in the project, merely commenting that, "It would've been great with Michael but Justin is my boy." He added: "I'm so glad that it turned out the way it did, because that was a wonderful experience for us to do that kinda work and for those songs to be brought to life."

Timberlake was similarly enlivened when he heard the demos and was given the chance to put his stamp on them. "For me, one of the cooler parts of this project, since we finished recording, has been gauging the surprise of people after they hear it," he said at the close of recording. "Even after the single ['Like I Love You'] came out and people were drawing all kinds of conclusions and saying, 'Check him, he's doing the Michael Jackson thing,' I thought, 'Just wait until you hear the rest of what we've got going on.'"

If the intention with *Justified* was to create a latterday version of the sort of polished, melodic funk-pop Quincy Jones created for Michael Jackson on 1979's *Off The Wall*, then it was a case of job done. The opening track, 'Señorita', with its cowbell and electric piano motif, was actually less Michael and more Stevie Wonder circa 'He's Misstra Know-It-All' or *Songs In The Key Of Life*. It was also a quintessential cool Neptunes production, effortless, breezy, almost cheekily suave as Timberlake offered shout-outs to his male audience ("Gentlemen, good night") and, chuckling, to the females ("Ladies... good morning") over a playful Latin beat.

It became the fourth single to be issued from *Justified* in July 2003, when it reached number 27 on the Hot 100 (it charted higher in Australia and New Zelaland, at number six and number four respectively).

Second track, 'Like I Love You', was the first song Timberlake and The Neptunes recorded together at Master Sound Recording Studios and Windmark Recording, Virginia Beach. It featured a rap verse from hip hop duo Clipse, soon to be key figures in The Neptunes story. Meanwhile, all the instrumentation – the clipped live drums and Castilian-sounding, rapidly strummed acoustic guitar – was courtesy of Hugo and Williams, and the song's vocal arrangement was provided by Williams together with Timberlake. A song about infatuation, it also functioned as a paean to pop music itself – there is a part in the song, four minutes in, where the music drops out save for a solitary synth bleep, and Timberlake breathily exclaims: "You know, I used to dream about this when I was a little boy. Never dreamed it would end up this way" – and then, with devastating precision, he drops the word "drums" and the beat comes back in. "It's kind of special, right?" he says at this point in 'Like I Love You': he could be telling the female subject of the song about his sexual prowess, but it could just as easily be referring to the heart-stopping techniques of The Neptunes.

'Like I Love You' was chosen as Timberlake's debut single and the lead single from *Justified*. According to Timberlake, there was "never any question" in his mind as to whether it would be the first release. "It sounded so original to me," he said, justifying his choice of collaborators for his debut solo venture. "And I kind of consider myself a new artist. This is a new beginning for me, so why call on some big-name hip hop artist when I could get somebody that feels new so it could feel like we were chomping at the bit at the same time?"

It received glowing reviews. *Rolling Stone* praised its "nasty funk rhythm on loud, live drums… tiny guitar strum and Timberlake's breathy, studied tenor; it's minimalism influenced by Michael Jackson. But a softer, harmony-and-hook-filled chorus sets it off, thus pleasing preteen girls and beat junkies alike." BBC Music called it a "sure bet for success" and "one of the best Neptunes productions this year". Chart-wise, it peaked at number 11 in the US, where it stayed for a total of 36 weeks. In the UK, it entered the Top 10 at number two in November 2002 and remained on the chart until February 2003. It would be nominated for Best Rap/Sung Collaboration at the 45th Grammy Awards.

The video, starring Timberlake as the smooth criminal in a variety of urban milieus, helped its commercial ascent and propelled *Justified* into the sales stratosphere – to date, it has had nearly 35 million views on YouTube. It featured a cameo from Pharrell – fast becoming one of his hallmarks, à la film director Alfred Hitchcock, who would almost always crop up, albeit for a split second, in his movies. In this one, Williams offered a few tantalising moments of body-popping, but it was definitely a case of less is more. It was electrifying.

"Only you caught that," he said, taken aback, when I met him for the *Guardian* in 2004 and noted his contribution to the 'Like I Love You' video. "It was, like, 'Woah, we did something.' That's what it was. You're the only person in the world who caught that. I just remember thinking, 'We're gonna fuck 'em up with this.'"

The third track on *Justified* was '(Oh No) What You Got', which was like a teen-pop version of Ma$e's 'Lookin' At Me', only with racy lyrics (it involves a young lady who, faced with the JT frame, suffers from wandering hands). 'Take It From Here' was a sultry, some might say slushy, ballad ("Girls are going to fall in love with that song," anticipated Chad Hugo) that Timberlake unexpectedly revealed was written under the influence of alternative country-rock act Mazzy Star, with a vocal performed in the style of Radiohead's Thom Yorke.

"I was thinking about Thom Yorke and Mazzy Star as I was singing that song," he said. "It's totally fresh and different. It's also completely me – and that's what counts most of all. There's a lot more to me than people have previously believed."

There were two further singles on the album. First was 'Cry Me A River', a collaboration with Timbaland bearing echoes of his collaborations with Aaliyah that included all manner of Arabian-tinged elements, even Gregorian chants. It concerned a brokenhearted man haunted by his past: Timberlake split up with Britney Spears prior to recording the album and it was alleged that some of the tracks addressed that broken romance. Chad Hugo said as much at the time, acknowledging that fans would likely read what they wanted to into some of the lyrics.

"There could be songs about that," he said. "Everyone incorporates their personal lives into their songs."

'Cry Me A River' was a Top Three in the States, Britain and Australia. The follow-up single, 'Rock Your Body', was a Neptunes team-up incorporating clavichord-emulating synths and a groove reminiscent of late-seventies disco, especially Jackson's *Off The Wall* and Chic's brilliant 1979 album, *Risqué*. It was certified gold in America and sold well around the world, although it did soundtrack a controversial moment later on when, during the 2004 Super Bowl, in a performance in which he was joined by Janet Jackson, Timberlake sang the lyric, "I'll have you naked by the end of this song" and promptly ripped off part of her outfit, briefly exposing her right breast on live television. Timberlake distanced himself from the ensuing media storm while Jackson faced considerable opprobrium. He later mused that "America's harsher on women...[and] unfairly harsh on ethnic people."

The remainder of *Justified* comprised the slinky Stevie Wonder-ful R&B of 'Nothin' Else', which could easily have been lifted off of one of Wonder's glorious mid-seventies albums; the splendid staccato strut of 'Last Night'; the slow jam 'Still On My Brain'; and the Timbaland-produced '(And She Said) Take Me Now', which did finally see Janet Jackson singing on a Neptunes tune, one in hock to Wonder's 'Superstition' right up to its bubbling Moog synth sounds. There was one more Timbaland track, 'Right For Me', and one further Neptunes cut, 'Let's Take A Ride'. The album concluded with weepie 'Never Again', a Brian McKnight co-write. It was probably the only weak spot on an otherwise immaculate collection, an attempt at a 'She's Out Of My Life', the famous ballad from *Off The Wall*.

Justified was generally received warmly in the press. In a four out of five star review *Rolling Stone* commended The Neptunes' production and noted that Timberlake had successfully "vaulted over the canyon to adulthood". *Slant* magazine decided that Timberlake was so well integrated he was effectively a third member of the Neptunes team. *Entertainment Weekly* wrote that *Justified* was "the ultramodern R&B-pop hybrid" that Michael Jackson's 2001 album *Invincible* should have been. *Stylus* magazine considered that it "paints a picture of a complicated young man, growing into adulthood", although *NME* was less convinced, calling Timberlake's lyrics "soppy platitudes that may or may not be about Britney".

The reviews may have been equivocal, but it was a triumph awards-wise, earning three American Music Award nominations, including Favorite Pop/Rock Album, Favorite Pop/Rock Male Artist and Fan Choice Award, and winning the award for Favorite Pop/Rock Album at the highly prestigious 45th Grammy Awards. And there was no denying its commercial performance: *Justified* debuted at number two on the *Billboard* 200, where it remained for 72 weeks, eventually selling four million copies in the States, while in the UK it debuted at number six, going on to claim the top spot for seven weeks and sell almost two million.

With *Justified* and all the other albums and singles they had produced, The Neptunes proved themselves highly effective facilitators of other people's work. Now all Williams and Hugo had to do was create something of their own.

CHAPTER 4

Run To The Sun

"N★*E*★*R*★*D is our heart and what we eat, shit and breathe"*
— Shay Haley

Pharrell Williams, with Chad Hugo, had already produced literally dozens of records – singles and albums – for other artists by the early part of the 21st century. And Pharrell himself had make sparkling cameos on singles by the likes of Mystikal and Jay-Z. The latter's 'I Just Wanna Luv U (Give It To Me)' was a particularly significant release, one that made evident The Neptunes' grip on turn-of-the-decade radio, rap or otherwise. Lifted off the 2000 album *The Dynasty: Roc La Familia*, it was a number 11 hit in the States and number 17 in the UK. That was the song that made Britney Spears realise she wanted to work with The Neptunes, so engaging was Williams' cool, airy falsetto and his and Hugo's cheekily languid funky beat. It was their magic touch that helped transform Britney from bubblegum-cute girl-next-door to X-rated sex nymphette; but it also gave Jay-Z his first number one on the hip hop/R&B *Billboard* chart.

Recorded at New York's Baseline Studios, 'I Just Wanna Luv U (Give It To Me)' was the moment they made the transition from supremely credible soundsmiths with both ears attuned to the beatgeist, to the premier pop producers on the planet. With its artificial clavichord sounds and spacious boom bap drums complete with additional layers of synthetic hand percussion, 'I Just Wanna Love U' sounded alien, "like robots from the future discovering funk" according to *Complex* magazine. The chorus featured vocals from Pharrell – his falsetto cries of "I just wanna laaaaaaav ya!" over The Neptunes' sparse yet insistent beat – as well as singing from Chad Hugo and Shay Haley, Williams' and Hugo's friend from their childhood days in Virginia (he was from Portsmouth, Missy Elliott's home town). It's entirely possible that this, with all three of them in the studio together, was when they decided that the three of them should get together to make their first album as N★E★R★D.

The name N★E★R★D had been kicking around since the early nineties at least, when they were still at high school. But now it was time to use it to put their personal stamp on the music industry in no uncertain terms. Au fait with technology since their childhood days messing around with Casio keyboards, N★E★R★D became increasingly competent across a range of instruments as time went on. Eventually, Williams would be responsible for lead vocals, piano/keyboards, drums and percussion; Hugo for lead guitar, piano/keyboards, saxophone, bass and backing vocals; and Haley for drums, percussion and backing vocals.

But the question as to where The Neptunes ended and N★E★R★D began became more difficult to answer on the release, in September 2001, of *In Search Of...*, the debut album by N★E★R★D. The credits stated that the album was produced by The Neptunes, for Star Trak Entertainment, a label founded by Williams and Hugo and a subsidiary of Virgin Records. To further muddy the waters, The Neptunes were closely associated with the studio whereas N★E★R★D was the name of the band who, during 2002-4, would earn a reputation as one of the fiercest rap-rock coalitions on the concert circuit. Indeed, at the Irving Plaza in New York in September 2002, N★E★R★D, with their backing band, Minneapolis' Spymob, came across like bona fide hip hop rockers. Williams was like a living bisection of the two lifestyles, with his baseball cap and chunky jewellery, while the musicians thrilled the mixed-race crowd. N★E★R★D's schizoid impulses were on show because they were entirely comfortable in the studio, performing with the same ease with which The Neptunes twiddled the controls over at the recording console. Distinguishing between one and the other was a complicated affair, made all the more confusing when *In Search Of...* was re-recorded and reissued in 2002 in a version jointly performed by members of Spymob.

"N★E★R★D is our heart and what we eat, shit and breathe," said Haley, trying to define the difference between the band and the production team. Haley was the most low-key member of the band – in an interview with *The Source* magazine, he admitted this was intentional, so keen was he to avoid such trappings of success as being mobbed by masses of fans or having to hire a bodyguard.

It was down to Chad Hugo to further shed light on the great N★E★R★D/Neptunes conundrum. "N★E★R★D stands for No One Ever Really Dies," he said. "We chose that name to keep it separate from the Neptunes entity: the Neptunes as producers, N★E★R★D as artists."

He and Williams even came up with a superhero analogy to help clarify the situation: The Neptunes, decided Hugo, were like Spiderman, while N★E★R★D were more Peter Parker.

"More personal, y'know?" he laughed. "None of the uh, wall-climbing business!"

In 2001, they were full of superhero analogies because in an interview with Britain's *Daily Telegraph*, Williams had this to say. "As producers, we're like Batman, a guy with a job to do," he told Ben Thompson, who marvelled at the tattoo, on his upper arms, approximating the Cistine chapel ceiling, and his T-shirt bearing the name of Canadian progressive rock gods Rush. "But as N★E★R★D we're more like Bruce Wayne. It's more like an individual with their own personality and feelings... and it's those emotions that the record should be selling... that, and the fact that the album is multi-metaphorical."

Later, in an attempt to make a clearer distinction, Williams proclaimed: "N★E★R★D is who we ARE, Neptunes is what we DO."

Beyond the moniker, the primary motivating factor for N★E★R★D was friendship – this was a creative endeavour undertaken by three boyhood pals who shared a postcode and a desire to think outside the rap/R&B box. "The first connection and foremost is that we're all friends," confirmed Pharrell.

The second crucial element for N★E★R★D was that they should be able to "push the creative envelope as far as the imagination takes us". And the third? "That the music," pronounced Williams, portentously, "is futuristic."

If The Neptunes were all about sonics, N★E★R★D had a wide-ranging musical ambit as well as a lyrical vision that could veer from concerns quotidian to matters cosmic. "Curiosity illuminates the correct path to anything in life," Williams mused in *Interview* magazine. "If you're not curious, that's when your brain is starting to die. And discovering, I think. That's what separates us from the other species – it's that we discover and pioneer."

In a rare interview, Haley offered a glimpse into life behind the scenes in N★E★R★D and the real-world nature of their relationship. "We definitely bump heads sometimes," he said.

"It's healthy for the relationship. When you're dealing with three different, strong personalities, a lot of times we're pretty much on the same wavelength in terms of creativity. Then there's times where somebody will just come out with an idea that just doesn't make sense for the movement. We have healthy debates and figure out a better plan that makes sense for the group. We're trying that extreme idea and seeing how it works."

He explained that all three N*E*R*Ds brought ideas to the table, writing-wise, even if he didn't necessarily get a credit on the record sleeves. "It varies," stated Haley, who also made reference to the notion of "pushing the envelope and doing new things".

"Chad," he added, stressing the idea of N*E*R*D as a collective, with more or less equal say, "might come up with an idea, or Pharrell or myself. You know, it all varies, but we all work together. Pharrell and Chad are definitely the maestros musically behind it but I'm forever going through the crates and the archives, always searching for new sounds and directions that we can go in. So we can be ahead of the curve. N*E*R*D doesn't necessarily have to fit with what's going on."

If it was hard to tell whether N*E*R*D were a side project of The Neptunes, or vice versa, certainly there was no doubt the money earned in their latter incarnation gave them the freedom to really stretch out and experiment – afforded them the courage to fly or die – with the former. It didn't matter what the commercial outcome was, because they had day jobs as two of the world's top producers to make sure they wouldn't starve.

Or, as Pharrell put it more poetically, "When you're making records for yourself, you already know who you are; you can go as far deep into music as you can go without running into time. You can hold your breath for as long as you can and then come up for air and then go dive into another part of the pool, another part of life."

In Search Of… – named after the US TV series about mysterious phenomena hosted by *Star Trek* legend Leonard Nimoy that ran from 1977 to 1982 – went some way towards providing an answer to the question: where did The Neptunes end and N★E★R★D begin? Even in its first incarnation – the one released in September 2001, featuring a washed-out green image of Shay Haley playing with his Playstation on the front cover, as opposed to the re-recorded and reissued March 2002 version bearing the (also green) bleached-out profiles of Williams, Hugo and Haley – it was a largely electronic affair. And yet this was quite different to the spartan, spacey, sinewy digital R&B of The Neptunes. It offered something new: a soul-rock hybrid with elements of jazz-pop, rap and electronica. Certainly they were the first black rock act of note since Living Colour in the late eighties.

That first version of N★E★R★D's debut had the feel of a suite, even a concept, albeit a warped one. There was an intro, but it came after the first track, 'Lapdance'. And there were skits at the end of three numbers. These involved Shay Haley encountering a couple of High School groupies in a locker room (at the end of 'Things Are Getting Better'), telephoning an escort (after 'Stay Together') and recording her orgiastic moaning (at the climax, literally, of 'Tape You'). It wasn't obvious what the overarching theme was, but musically *In Search Of…* was a sort of 2001 update of Stevie Wonder's celestial soul, only with a gritty hip hop edge. On the other hand, despite the proliferation of synths and paucity of guitars, it had the punch and dynamism of a black rock album – no wonder Pharrell Williams was sporting an AC/DC T-shirt on the back cover. Nowhere did this ring more true than on opening track 'Lapdance', which featured singer Vita and rapper Lee Harvey. The buzzing synth – "like a wasp in your earhole", according to writer Simon Reynolds – assumed the role of an electric guitar riff, to the extent that subsequently the track was described variously as "funk rock" and "rap metal". The lyric, meanwhile, made connections between strippers and politicians, and the video found the three members of N★E★R★D surrounded by gyrating semi-naked females, which drew some flak, although it was nothing compared to the controversy that would, in 2013, be caused by the video to Robin Thicke's Pharrell-penned 'Blurred Lines'. 'Lapdance' was a thrilling introduction to *In Search Of…*, even if its intentions were unclear.

'Intro', confusingly the second track, further muddied the waters. Most of its dreamy 75 seconds comprised baby gurgles, cricket chirps and an abstract wash of synths. "Hey, it's me, your subconscious speaking," announced Pharrell. "We are the dreamers – and as long as we dream we will never die. You know why? Because No One Ever Really Dies." So far, so ethereal, only for the magical mood to be punctured by Williams leering: "Hey, baby. Me, Chad and Shay want to squeeze your titties."

On 'Things Are Getting Better', Pharrell demanded, "Check it out, bitch." Giving him the benefit of the doubt, it was as likely an entreaty to N★E★R★D's rivals to investigate their music as it was a misogynist put-down. It had an unusual rhythm, neither rock nor R&B but somewhere in between, melodic and jazzily mellifluous, only with moments of raunch, like Steely Dan jamming with The Stooges. Pharrell's voice was so sweet and seductive it served as a mocking counterpoint to the title. After the skit in which two giggly girls spied Haley and enthused about his outsized nose, there was 'Brain', a neat subversion of the old adage about liking someone for their looks: "Do I really love you, or do I really love your brain?" It was a theme that ran throughout Williams' music and musings: the importance of intelligence in choosing a mate (although it has also been read as a cheeky ode to fellatio). 'Provider' transitioned between slow acoustic bluesy strums and gentle, dreamy bossa nova (Pharrell was a fan of Sergio Mendes and

Brasil 66's jazzy, loungey easy-listening). Ever empathetic, in the song Williams told the tale of a drug dealer whose only recourse as a family man was to risk his life peddling drugs on the street. The final 45 seconds were sheer aural bliss as Williams assumed the role of the torn protagonist: "What am I supposed to do?" he whispered, presumably addressing his wife. "I love you." The song became the third and final single from the album in 2002, when it managed to gain minor popularity in Europe, charting in the Netherlands and Sweden. In the UK, it was released as a double A-side with a re-release of 'Lapdance', peaking at number 20. It came with a video in which Williams and Hugo rode around with a bike gang and Pusha T of Clipse played a drug dealer.

After the rapture, some rage: 'Truth Or Dare' featured Kelis, and would have fit quite nicely on her album, *Kaleidoscope*, as a companion piece to 'Caught Out There'. Paced like a futuristic foxtrot, its staccato beat was accompanied by a series of warnings such as "welcome to the fast lane". The attention to dynamics and drama was superb. "Come on, come on," implored Williams as Kelis demanded, "Baby, shake it up!" and Pusha T rapped in his inimitable style. In a typical move for N★E★R★D, who evidently suffered from ADHR&B, there was a diversion into soft-rock territory halfway through before returning to the central thrust. To keep things symmetrical, the song returned to blissful soft-rock mode at the end, with some airy "yeah, yeah, yeahs" from Williams et al sounding like a 21st century Isley Brothers. The mix of savage and soothing was becoming a N★E★R★D trademark. 'Run To The Sun' was exquisite astral soul with eco-conscious lyrics about the ocean and feeling "embarrassed for mankind" – in terms of agenda and atmosphere, it was so Marvin Gaye circa *What's Going On* or Stevie Wonder circa *Innervisions* or *Fulfillingness' First Finale*, it wasn't true. On 'Stay Together' the backwards keyboard sounds were intriguingly Beatles-esque, but the track just didn't have a melodic point, unusually for N★E★R★D. As such it was the one weak moment on the album (which is why it was handy when, on the 2002 rework/reissue, they made it the final track, so you could just switch off the CD after the penultimate tune, 'Bobby James', without it spoiling the flow).

After the skit in which Haley telephoned to hire a prostitute, there was 'Baby Doll', all clavinet, twangy guitar, lounge harmonies and off-beat keyboard licks whose insistent infectiousness recalled late-seventies Todd Rundgren or Hall & Oates, only given a Pharrell twist as he proclaimed the object of his affections "my alien". Not for nothing did Williams, in the *Washington Post*, declare himself a "chord fanatic", in an article in which he expressed his love of Earth, Wind & Fire and Steely Dan. He was a sucker for what he called "fearless melodies", by which he presumably meant those chord sequences that connoted tenderness and accessibility.

'Tape You', in which Williams convinced his girlfriend to appear in a porno, was somewhat overlong but enlivened (if you liked that kind of thing) by its sleazy Moog sounds and almost three minutes of orgasmic moaning and panting over cheesy skinflick-soundtrack strings. 'Am I High', featuring Malice, the other half of Clipse, was like thugged-out muzak, or a slow-motion dream sequence from a gangsta movie with the quality of a hallucination. 'Rock Star' would be the track that would change the most on version two of the album – here it was more spacious and synthy, still urgent and sharp but not quite the full-on attack that it would become. It was released as the second single from *In Search Of...*, performing better than predecessor, 'Lapdance', in the UK, where it peaked at number 15, despite lacking an accompanying video (there was one shot by renowned director Hype Williams, but it was shelved and remains unreleased). It also became the group's first single to chart in Australia and was used on the soundtracks to various films, TV shows and video games. They left the best till last: all phased falsetto and swooning chorus, 'Bobby James' was aural ambrosia, a song about a teen drug casualty and shoplifter that may have been the most alluring song about the narcotic netherworld since Curtis Mayfield's 'Freddie's Dead'. It closed with two minutes of sax and synth-fuelled easy listening, like the theme to *Shaft* if it had been written not by Isaac Hayes but by Burt Bacharach. Again, the POV was set to empathetic: *In Search Of...*, give or take the odd sex interlude, recalled the seventies heyday of conscious soul, positing Pharrell not as a libidinous loverman but a sociopolitically aware visionary.

"N★E★R★D... well, they're on some kind of early-seventies cosmic/social conscience trip, harking back to *What's Going On/ Innervisions/Harvest For The World*," wrote Simon Reynolds in his review of *In Search Of...* for *Uncut* magazine, which made it Album Of The Month. "Williams, in particular, seems intent on Really Saying Something, bringing back Content to the sonically radical but lyrically visionless black pop culture of the day." In a four-star review, *Rolling Stone* decreed it "part Timbaland, part Afrika Bambaataa, and part *Star Trek* on ecstasy." Robert Christgau of *The Village Voice* awarded it an A– grade, describing the contents as "annoyingly catchy". In another four-star review, *Q* magazine – which made it one of its top 50 albums of 2001 in its year-end issue – hailed it "a striking escape from mere genre... A swaggering, rock-friendly counterpoint to the likes of OutKast. And no less essential, either." *Vibe* called it "a complete departure, but with aural candy this flavourful, who cares?" *NME* gave it eight out of 10 and proclaimed it "awash with fuzzy-warm highs, hazy cosmic visions and exquisite ripples in the fabric of R&B as we know it." *Trouser Press* went furthest in its estimation: "Not since the eighties heyday of Prince and the Revolution has anyone made a funk-rock record as catchy, strange, filthy and exhilarating as *In Search Of...*"

Nevertheless, for all the glowing reviews for *In Search Of...*, there was a feeling in the N★E★R★D camp that it was insufficiently different to their work as The Neptunes, and that it needed tightening up. Another reason mooted for the re-recording of the album is that it was fundamentally wrong-headed. There had been a vocal contingent of hip hop writers from publications such as America's influential *XXL* who were so hostile towards the album and its daring fusion of smooth seventies FM radio tropes with harsh hip hop beats that it was decided – not long after the record had been shipped to stores and music magazines in Europe – to cancel the release and re-record the songs from scratch with a live rock band: Minnesota's Spymob, whose unreleased album for Epic had fallen into Pharrell Williams' hands and given him the idea for a live, energised version of the digitised melodies, grooves and bleeps of the original *In Search Of...*

It was crucial that N★E★R★D got it right: this was, after all, the first official foray of the band spin-off of one of the best-known production teams around. Still, it made for a great back-story to the release, making it seem even more like an event. And so version one was consigned to the dumper – it remains a very rare collectors' item to this day – while the second iteration came in a different sleeve and featured a different track listing (mainly in terms of ordering) and missed the skits at the end of three tracks, and the 'Intro'.

Overall, it had a rockier, looser feel, with greater use of live drums, piano and guitars, played by Spymob (following the making of this version, Williams and Hugo learned to play the guitar, and mostly played their own instruments). This more urgent, compact *In Search Of...* was more achievable in a concert context and allowed the group to tour and play live as N★E★R★D more easily (it was later released, in 2005, in a third iteration, as a 5.1 surround sound DVD-Audio edition, largely based on the 2002 release, only with slightly different mastering).

'Lapdance' was tougher than the original recording of the track, almost approaching thrash metal, and already by 'Things Are Getting Better' it was possible to tell the two versions of the album apart: this was more live, less layered and lush, more spontaneous and free, although kudos to the band for being able to even approach the louche intricacy of the original here. Now, the song rocked harder, but it also had more "swing". On 'Brain' the music was more upfront in the mix, and there was less of a honeyed glaze. 'Provider' was arguably even more affecting, especially knowing that the tempo shifts and transitions were being handled by musicians not machines. On 'Truth Or Dare' it became evident that the drums were the key re-recorded elements on the album, and there was a clunkiness that made it seem less pristine but arguably more exciting for it. 'Tape You' and 'Baby Doll' throbbed in a way that the originals didn't. 'Bobby James' and 'Run To The Sun' were as lovely as ever.

Of all the tracks on the re-recorded *In Search Of...*, 'Rock Star' was the most startlingly different, with powerful thrash-style eruptions and juddering blasts of guitar, bass and drums (the UK version of the album had as a bonus track a house remix of the track from Jason Nevins that ironed out the rhythmic idiosyncrasies, but had a propulsive energy all its own). It was here that the album makeover made most sense, the new mix's beefed-up sound bringing the track to life, its enormous crashing drums giving authority to Pharrell's rowdy chant of, "You can't be me, I'm a rock star!" The music seemed designed for mosh pits.

Spin magazine suggested that N★E★R★D were "critiquing hip hop from the inside" on 'Rock Star' and 'Lapdance', but they were also oblique comments on rap-metal and its attendant culture. Hugo, Haley and Williams were having their cake and eating it: slyly taking sideswipes at clubs that wanted to enlist them as members.

A bid for true artistry and credibility, the re-recorded *In Search Of...* was hailed as one of the most intriguing, adventurous albums of the new decade. It earned a rave review in *Spin*, which gave it eight out of 10 and praised its "ace genre-mashing". The magazine especially warmed to the new, rockier sound, which it decided made it seem "weirder, punching up the rock that was merely implicit on the previous version. That's 'rock' as in rap-rock, alt-rock and Paisley Park psych-rock, even country rock." RapReviews.com called it "a musical experiment – a joyride for the Neptunes to go crazy on" while *Alternative Press* decided that it bore "a surprising similarity to modern metal" and Mojo fell for its "unique fusions of harmony-led AOR... Sly and Funkadelic, fragile singing and Eminem-esque raps, conscious seventies soul, eighties synth-pop and Hendrix-esque rock".

It fared well at the box office, too, albeit not in quite the same quantities as some of their collaborations with big-name stars. *In Search Of...* peaked at number 56 and sold 603,000 copies in the US, meaning it was certified Gold. It was also awarded the second annual Shortlist Music Prize, an accolade given to albums released in the US with sales of 500,000 or below at the time of nomination – it beat the likes of Björk, The Flaming Lips, DJ Shadow, Aphex Twin and CeeLo Green. On the back of its success – and The Neptunes' concurrent productions – Williams won the 2002 Songwriter of the Year award from Broadcast Music Inc. (BMI), which tracks radio airplay (he'd won it the previous year, too). Not to be outdone, Chad Hugo received a Songwriter of the Year award for 2002 from The American Society of Composers, Authors and Publishers (ASCAP).

If *In Search Of...* was one of the very best albums of the early-noughties, then 'Grindin'', by the Virginia rap duo Clipse, was one of the very best singles. Released in May 2002, it was one of The Neptunes' most striking productions, and remains so to this day: not for nothing did *Complex* magazine, in 2012, vote it at number 20 in its list of the 100 Greatest Hip Hop Beats Of All Time, and at number one in its ranking of the best Neptunes beats ever.

Clipse – brothers Gene "No Malice" Thornton (formerly known as "Malice") and Terrence "Pusha T" Thornton – were born in the Bronx and moved to Virginia Beach, although they remained, in many ways, dispossessed New York rappers, their music evincing the influence of the Big Apple and its rap music of the eighties and early nineties. Following a brief stint making music as Jarvis, the pair formed Clipse in 1992. Not long after, they were introduced to Pharrell Williams, who was apparently impressed with their lyrical prowess. Eventually, he managed to secure a deal for them with Elektra Records in 1997, and they set to work, with The Neptunes, on their debut album, *Exclusive Audio Footage*. In 1999, they issued what ought to have been the lead single, 'The Funeral', which sampled Blood, Sweat & Tears' 'God Bless The Child' and came accompanied with a video featuring No Malice and Pusha T at their own funeral, dressed in white suits, the rest of the congregants (including Williams and Hugo) in black suits. 'The Funeral' had been written in the aftermath of the deaths of several of Pusha T's friends.

"It seemed like we were going to an abnormal amount of funerals all at once," he told *Complex*. "So we decided to make a song eulogising ourselves."

Unfortunately, despite both song and video being praised by rap fans, Elektra deemed it insufficiently commercial and decided to shelve the recording of the Neptunes-helmed *Exclusive Audio Footage* and Clipse were released from their record contract.

Luckily, Williams and Hugo had more faith in the pair, and so, in early 2001, they signed to Arista Records via the recently established Star Trak Entertainment imprint. In August 2002, Clipse released their debut album proper, *Lord Willin'*. It was a veritable Neptunes-fest, Hugo and Williams conjuring a slew of their most infectious beats and tunes while ingeniously providing the Thornton brothers with an appropriately edgy context for their tales of drug dealing and sleazy street life.

Such was the predilection on the part of the general public for rap *vérité* with a cartoonishly pleasing musicality that the album debuted at number one on *Billboard*'s hip hop chart and number four on the *Billboard* Hot 200. It sold 122,000 copies in its first week of release and was certified Gold by October 2002. Within five years, it had shifted almost a million units, on the strength of anthems such as 'Virginia', 'Ego', 'Gangsta Lean' and 'Let's Talk About It', and its singles, 'When The Last Time' (which Complex described as sounding like "a party on a Vulcan spacecraft", highlighting Neptunes' ability "to make engaging music that challenges as much as it reassures"), 'Ma, I Don't Love Her', 'Hot Damn', and particularly, 'Grindin''.

A Top 30 hit in July 2002, "coke rap" landmark 'Grindin'' was the quintessential Clipse track, and one of a handful of Neptunes beats that merit the epithet "iconic". Obviously it was quite far from the fare that they produced for some of their poppier clientele, but that doesn't mean 'Grindin'' was inaccessible. Quite the opposite. Designed for blasting out of stereos in cars, preferably the low-riding variety, minimalist yet futuristic, with a refrain that stuck in the brain from the first time you heard it, 'Grindin'' was swaggeringly audacious. It had a speaker-pummelling immediacy, thanks to its utter sparseness, allowing you to hear in total clarity the forceful drums, the crisp handclaps right upfront in the mix, not forgetting the eerily high vocals, the artfully coruscating lyrics ("From days I wasn't able, there was always 'caine"), and the unexpected but effective addition of the woodblocks – yes, woodblocks. It was like a classic, brutally stripped-down eighties hip hop track, updated for the Neptunes generation, and as such it set the tone for such future productions as Snoop Dogg's 'Drop It Like It's Hot'.

Pusha T recalled the moment he first heard the backing track, which came with a friendly threat.

"I remember being at home and Pharrell saying, 'Listen, I got this record and if you don't come to the studio in the next 15 minutes, I'm gonna give this record to Jay-Z.' And he just knows that it would burn me up inside if he did something like that. I'm very territorial about Neptunes' production. I'll leave text messages, voice messages, and emails of pure disgust and disrespect when they give away records that I feel like I should have had."

Apparently, he made it to the studio with two minutes to spare. Now the only challenge was, how to rhyme to such an unorthodox beat?

"It was so unorthodox that I couldn't really catch it," said Pusha T.

Explained Chad Hugo of his and Williams' back-to-the-future strategy with 'Grindin'': "We just wanted to strip it down – just a break[beat] and a rapper. That's how hip hop was born. We just wanted to bring that element back to the music scene."

'Grindin''s chart position – it peaked at number 30 – didn't quite reflect its dominance of radio that summer. Its impact was definitely felt among cognoscenti, not just around the time of its release but in the years to come: the song was listed at number 27 on Pitchfork Media's Top 500 songs of the 2000s, and at number 84 in *Rolling Stone*'s best songs of the decade. As for website Fancy Sounds, in 2011 it simply proclaimed it "the king of all Neptunes beats".

It had some competition, though. In 2001-2 alone, among their many collaborations, The Neptunes produced or remixed – lent their magic to – half a dozen records that emphasised their astonishing versatility and extraordinary consistency when it came to coming up with memorable musical backdrops and rhythms. In 2001, they remixed Daft Punk's 'Harder, Better, Faster, Stronger' from the French duo's *Discovery* album. It was a mouthwatering combination, involving the Parisian maestros of electronic dance and their Virginian counterparts, one that anticipated by a dozen years the world-shakingly triumphant collaboration that was 2013's 'Get Lucky'.

Another early glimpse, from 2001, of a globally successful team-up was the one between Messrs Williams and Hugo and No Doubt. Three years ahead of Gwen Stefani's Neptunes-penned 'Hollaback Girl' she recorded 'Hella Good' with her old ska-punk band, who by the turn of the decade were not quite the commercial force that they were circa 1996's 'Don't Speak'. Luckily, Pharrell and Chad were on hand with their Midas touch to re-ignite their fire and make them seem interesting again. 'Hella Good' was an abrupt change of pace, style, everything for the band from Anaheim, California. An electro-rock-disco delight, it drew on such dance-floor staples as Michael Jackson's 'Billie Jean' (for the beat), Lipps Inc's 'Funky Town' (for the synth bleeps) and Madonna's 'Into The Groove' (for the ecstatic chorus). It also had a shuddering electronic bass pulse that brought to mind Kraftwerk in the ghetto with Afrika Bambaataa, and a healthy dose of rock in the form of some slashing guitar reminiscent of INXS' 'Need You Tonight', plus some of the guitar crunch on the chorus of ZZ Top. As the song reached its dizzying peak – all synth sirens, Stefani's heavy breathing, and a succulent, succinct guitar solo – it occurred that 'Hella Good', a number 13 US hit, would have been one of the better tracks on N★E★R★D's *In Search Of...* or Kelis' *Kaleidoscope*. Praise indeed.

Stefani made a cameo appearance on 'Perfect Day', a track from Kelis' second album, *Wanderland*. The latter was another

Neptunes-helmed affair from 2001 and another demonstration of Williams and Hugo's ability to sustain their ideas over the length of an LP. It spawned one UK hit in 'Young, Fresh 'n' New', reaching number 32 in September 2001, which was described by *Blender* magazine as "a delirious four and a half minutes of rasping, intergalactic funk which sounds as if it was recorded in the engine room of the U.S.S. Enterprise". As for the album, it received plaudits such as "clever, exhilarating and original" and "The Neptunes' most adventurous work to date" (*The Guardian*), and "Kelis' brash blend of Curtis Mayfield soul, techno-Zeppelin funk, Jobim-lite bossa nova, and ultrasmooth R&B shows a more coherent artistry than many recent boundary-busting experiments" (*Entertainment Weekly*).

In 2002, The Neptunes produced three seminal singles. First there was Busta Rhymes' 'Pass The Courvoisier, Part II', from February 2002, which helped reactivate the rapper's career after a couple of years in the doldrums. It was a version of a track that originally just featured P Diddy and appeared on Rhymes' fifth album, *Genesis*. With Pharrell added to the remix, and accompanied by a video inspired by 'Harlem Nights' and 'Rush Hour 2', the song reached number 11 on the US *Billboard* Hot 100. With its frantic mess of 12-string guitars, its brass section, bongos, crowd hubbub, and a backing track featuring Pharrell and Diddy yelling at each other, this was, as *Complex* magazine put it, "a party song that actually sounds like a party".

If 'Pass The Courvoisier, Part II' demonstrated The Neptunes' facility with rap, Nelly's April 2002 single 'Hot In Herre' proved their complete command of R&B and electronic funk. The lead single from the St Louis rapper/singer's second album, *Nellyville*, 'Hot In Herre' parlayed a supremely infectious summer paean to stripping off (the two "rr"s signalled that the club in the song was really, extra hot) out of a series of Neil Young ('There's A World'),

Nancy Sinatra (her cover of 'As Tears Go By') and Chuck Brown ('Bustin' Loose') samples. It reached number one in the US and Canada and number four in the UK and won Nelly a Grammy in 2003 for Best Male Rap Solo Performance. It was at once highly unorthodox and supremely infectious.

"I did that in L.A... I remember 'cause Busta [Rhymes] was in the same studio and he came through and he heard the beat and you know how Busta is, you know he's over the top. He's like, 'Yo, god! What is that sound?!!?!?'" laughed Nelly, reminiscing about the recording of the track in a 2010 interview with *XXL* magazine. "What is that sound coming from here, god? Oh my, god! Pharrell, where was that beat at? Where was that? You were hiding that from me!' It was a little unorthodox for the time..."

The third in a triptych of sublime 2002 recordings by The Neptunes was 'Beautiful', from Snoop Dogg's 2002 album *Paid Tha Cost To Be Da Bo$$* (the single itself wasn't actually released until January 2003). Featuring Pharrell and Charlie Wilson, from seventies/eighties electro-funk hit-makers The Gap Band, of 'Oops Up Side Your Head' fame, 'Beautiful' was a Latin-ish delight, with its stuttering rhythm, piquant guitar figure, light bongo taps and Pharrell's typically airy vocal melody over a trademark spacious Neptunes arrangement. Before you even heard it you could tell Snoop and Pharrell would be flying directly to Brazil for the video shoot. You could also tell it would be a Top 10 hit all around the world.

And still Williams had barely begun to scratch the surface of what he could achieve.

CHAPTER 5

Breakout

'The funny thing is, I don't feel like a star"

— Pharrell Williams

There were several signs, in 2003, of Pharrell Williams' increasing cultural penetration. You could, for example, see The Neptunes' remix of The Rolling Stones' 'Sympathy For The Devil' as evidence of their acceptance at the highest levels of the rock hierarchy. Certainly, remixes of Jagger and Co's work were few and far between. Williams' desire to extend his brand into areas non-musical were apparent in his Billionaire Boys Club and Ice Cream clothing lines. And his and Hugo's desire to foster new talent and retain control of their own work could be seen in Star Trak Entertainment. The label had been formed in 2001, initially partly funded by Arista Records in a joint venture. Star Trak signees included Clipse, Kelis, Vanessa Marquez, Fam-Lay, N★E★R★D and Spymob, the band who provided backing instruments for N★E★R★D's debut album, *In Search Of....* In 2003, Star Trak enjoyed a number one LP hit when they issued

The Neptunes Present... Clones. A further blurring of the boundary between N★E★R★D and The Neptunes, it was a kind of cross between a prototype mix-tape, a greatest hits compilation and an album proper, featuring as it did tracks by a variety of different artists, several of which already were, or eventually became, singles. All 18 tracks were produced by Chad Hugo and Pharrell Williams, aka The Neptunes. It was released on August 19, 2003 and achieved first-week sales of 249,000 copies in the US, where it debuted at number one and was certified Gold. The album featured four singles: 'Light Your Ass On Fire' by Busta Rhymes, 'Hot Damn' by Clipse, 'It Blows My Mind' by Snoop Dogg and, perhaps most memorably, 'Frontin'', the first official solo single by Pharrell.

The latter, about putting up a false facade, featured Jay-Z, and although it was accompanied by a declaration from Williams that it was a one-off – that he was a producer rather than an artist in his own right – it actually launched what would become an amazingly successful solo career, one that culminated, in 2013-14, with the global mega-hit 'Happy'. 'Frontin'' itself didn't exactly perform shabbily: it was the 34th best-selling song of 2003 in the US, it peaked at number five on the *Billboard* Hot 100 and, in the UK, at number six, where it spent 10 weeks within the Top 75, and it was Pharrell's biggest solo hit until 'Happy'. It enjoyed a considerable afterlife, too, courtesy of numerous cover versions: it was a bonus track on the US release of British pop-jazz artist Jamie Cullum's 2003 album *Twentysomething* and, released as a single, it reached number 12 in the UK. In fact, Williams was so impressed by Cullum's take on his work that it led to him signing a recording contract with Williams' Star Trak. 'Frontin'' was also covered live by Maroon 5, and, as late as 2014, UK garage duo Disclosure remixed the song. If Pharrell seriously had no intention of pursuing a side career as a solo artist, then this would have been an incredible one-off.

The Neptunes ended 2003 with a triumph for themselves and their long-standing collaborator Kelis Rogers: a worldwide pop smash with a track from Kelis' third album, *Tasty*. It was called 'Milkshake' and it was payback for Williams and Hugo, who up to this point had had little success with their productions for Kelis outside of 1998's scorned lover anthem 'Caught Out There'. 'Milkshake', by contrast, was more than a critical rave. It did indeed become one of Williams' and Hugo's most highly acclaimed compositions and productions, but this time it sold in vast quantities. Not that it was an obvious hit. A thoroughly idiosyncratic affair, after four opening beats it launched into the chorus, a monotone series of deadpan declarations from Kelis over a squiggly sub-bass synth. Then there was the exotic bongo pattern and high-pitched triangle sound. If ever there was evidence of the general public's capacity to embrace the experimental, it was 'Milkshake' – it reached number three in the States and number two in the UK, remaining her biggest hit in both territories to date. Williams and Hugo had other excellent tracks on *Tasty* – 'Flashback', 'Protect My Heart', 'Sugar Honey Iced Tea', 'Rolling Through The Hood' – but 'Milkshake' was the one that drew most attention. It appeared in a slew of movies, including *Mean Girls* and *Date Movie*, and in TV shows such as *Family Guy*, *The Simpsons*, *Nip/Tuck* and *Ugly Betty*, proof of its cultural penetration.

Discussing the meaning behind 'Milkshake', amid observations that it was a sexual image, Kelis toned things down by declaring: "A milkshake is the thing that makes women special." In the December 12, 2004 edition of *Observer Music Magazine*, she furthered that 'Milkshake' "means whatever people want it to; it was just a word we came up with on a whim, but then the song took on a life of its own". In 2010, still discussing what was without doubt her most famous track, she asserted her belief that it was hugely influential on a generation of female artists. She described it as a game-changer, one of those rare pieces of music that draws a line between those who came before and those who came after.

"I mean, you kind of have to be retarded to deny that it literally changed female vocalists," she said.

Oddly, given the success of 'Milkshake', it was around this time that rumours began emerging that Kelis and The Neptunes had had a falling out. She told a reporter that her working relationship with Williams and Hugo and their Star Trak imprint had been marred by tension.

"Star Trak and I have a weird relationship," she revealed. "There's some tension right now. They're a new label. They're confused as to what they're doing. It's hard when a label head [Williams] is artist and CEO. You have to pick one because one is gonna suffer. The label is suffering and the artists are suffering."

Kelis went so far as to say she believed Williams and Hugo despised her. "I think they hate me," she said. "They just do crazy shit sometimes. We don't talk. I haven't talked to them in a while. I really don't have any hate [towards them], and I'm not bitter. I've been down with them and I support them. I signed with them because I think they're some of the most talented people in the game. I give credit where credit is due."

She couldn't exactly explain the depth of negative feeling, although part of the problem, in her estimation, was that she was "excluded from everything". "They hate on me every possible chance they can. It does not stop," she carped, going on to describe Star Trak as "the most uninvolved label I've seen in my life".

By early 2004, Arista Records had severed ties with Star Trak Entertainment, which proceeded to ink a new distribution deal with EMI's Virgin Records. The first release from this deal was *Fly Or Die*, the second album by N★E★R★D. It didn't fare any better than its predecessor, commercially, and got a mixed reception from the press, ranging from the ecstatic – *Uncut* magazine deemed it a pop-rock triumph, the daring missing link between XTC and EW&F – to entertaining crucifixions such as the one from Pitchfork, which decided that "*Fly Or Die* finds the safe middle ground between Adam Ant's rumbling Burundi-drummed new wave pop, Earth, Wind & Fire's digital elevator nightmare *Raise!*, and Lenny Kravitz's Folgers granule guitars", adding, amusingly, that their prog R&B was "like Nile Rodgers producing Gentle Giant".

The author of this book was more in the "pro-, Pharrell can do no wrong" camp and so earned a commission by the *Guardian* newspaper to interview Williams. It turned out to be one of the fuller interviews he has given. I spent a whole day in his company, quite unusual, even unprecedented, for a star of his stature – to put things into perspective, generally for an artist of Williams' ilk, you are allowed, at most, an hour in a hotel room, often under the watchful eye of a press officer or manager/minder. In this instance, on the other hand, I joined him as he and his entourage moved freely from his hotel room to the BBC to MTV, all the while travelling with him in his limo as he switched venues. In addition, I had access to his brother, who had joined with him on tour. Not all of the interview(s) and observations recorded that day made their way into print. And so the following contains exclusive, previously unseen material; taken in total, the near 6,000-word encounter amounts to one of the most in-depth meetings with Williams to date, offering some insight into his mental state at the time, his aspirations, even frustrations.

It was February 13, 2004, late morning at the St Martin's Lane hotel in London's Covent Garden, that I first met Pharrell. I noted at the time that it would have been hard to guess that the sleepy-eyed, pretty vacant, young black American who greeted me in room 101, stumbling away from the unmade bed to be interviewed by the *Guardian*, was probably the most important man in music at that time.

I say that because of his status as one half of The Neptunes, who had up to that point enjoyed a staggering run of success, with hits provided for everyone from Britney Spears, Beyoncé and Justin Timberlake to Jay-Z, Kelis and Snoop Dogg. Then there was his band N★E★R★D, whose subtly experimental rhythms and sunkissed synth-soul, digital funk and hard rock produced 2001's exceptional *In Search of...*, with a soon to be released follow-up called *Fly Or Die*. Factor in also his burgeoning solo career (his debut 'Frontin'' was a hit the year before), his Star Trak record label and Billionaire Boys Club clothing company, "not to mention," I added, "the sort of pin-up appeal that induces swooning fits in women of all races, creeds and ages", and here was one seriously powerful, credible, in-demand individual.

I asked Williams whether he accepted his status as the Midas of the music industry?

"No way, no," he sighed, pulling his combat sweat-top hood up over his head, still floored by jet lag. He lifted his pink, grey and white sneakers onto the sofa so he could stretch out. They were his design, in tandem with renowned Japanese artist Nigo, part of a run of clothing that he gave the name Ice Cream. Why? "Because ice and cream are two things that run the world," he explained. "The jewellery – the ice – the diamonds; and the cream is the cash. I wanted to be the first guy to put that on the kids' feet."

Pharrell yawned, and his whole body shuddered. Not only was he jet-lagged, he had spent the previous night partying till the early hours at London clubs Brown's and the Rex.

"The funny thing is, I don't feel like a star," he continued in that soft, seductive, singsong voice of his. Surely he must have had some inkling of his stature – after all, the paparazzi, much to his annoyance, had already discovered where he was staying, which was why, when I saw him outside the hotel after this interview, he was wearing his hood up again, but this time with a matching combat cap, and a scarf to hide his face. "Being in newspapers, being rumoured to be messing with this girl or messing with that girl – that's not what I got into this business for."

It was pretty certain that, for Williams, the recording studio was his retreat, one that served him well. Did he know that, in August 2003, a survey of British radio found that nearly 20 percent of tracks played were Neptunes productions?

"Thank you," he said in response to the regurgitated statistic, "that's quite a compliment."

It wasn't a compliment, it was a fact. On the cover of *The Neptunes Present ... Clones*, the 2003 LP featuring the rap elite (Busta Rhymes, N.O.R.E., Clipse, Ludacris, Nelly), Williams and Hugo were pictured, arms folded, bestriding the universe like twin musical colossi. Had they come to save mankind from terrible, manufactured karaoke pop idols?

"No," he replied, "we just want to make good music." Did he not believe that he was on a mission?

"Nah," he said. "Credit isn't to be taken, it's to be given."

With his dominance of the pop business, did he consider himself one of the most important players in the game?

"No way," he replied, emphatically. "No."

Fly Or Die, he explained, was about nothing less than "the evolution of man. We can be optimistic – fly – or become extinct – die. We gotta keep moving forward." Then 31, and every inch the hip hop space cadet, Williams informed me that, during his flight over from the States the day before, he was reading *The Da*

Vinci Code, Dan Brown's 2003 novel which, according to one reviewer, concerned "secret codes, elaborate technology, pagan sex orgies, pre-Christian fertility cults, Gnostic Gospels, brutal murders and feminist theory".

"It's about the re-emergence of the Holy Grail," Williams furthered, "what that means to many different religions and its political effect since the day of Christ." How, I wondered, would Williams define his own religious beliefs?

"I'm Christian," he admitted, adding that he rarely attended church ("I ain't been in so long, man"), but that didn't affect his beliefs. "God knows my heart," he declared. "I have conversations with God a few times every day." Rich, successful, did he thank the Lord on a regular basis? "Absolutely," he said. "I spend more time thanking him for the shit I don't have than the things I do got."

How did he reconcile his enormous wealth with his spirituality, his desire, as he puts it, not to get "caught up in worldly things"?

"I don't worry about things like that," he said, dismissively. Later, he had on round his neck a gold chain and pendant so chunky it hardly seemed real; it was a bling contrast to his otherwise down-to-earth skater-boy apparel. Did his wealth ever make him feel guilty?

"Well, I'm a philanthropist, too," he parried. Indeed, in 2002 he recorded a charity record called 'American Prayer' with Bono of U2 and Dave Stewart, formerly of Eurythmics.

"It was to do with [Nelson] Mandela," he explained, "because he's getting older. We wanted to pay tribute to him."

Did he meet Bono?

"Yeah, he's a great guy. We were in the studio, in New York. And Beyoncé was there."

Did you go partying afterwards?

harrell Williams at the MTV Europe Music Awards in Barcelona, November 14, 2002, when he was one of the celebrity guest presenters.

Pharrell at high school, where he took part in a talent show and was discovered by R&B supremo Teddy Riley.

Performing with Jay-Z, Damon Dash and The Roots on MTV Unplugged at the MTV studios in New York City, November 1 2001. SCOTT GRIES/IMAGEDIRECT

At the Shoreline Amphitheater in Mountain View CA, June 14, 2002. TIM MOSENFELDER/GETTY IMAGES

Pharrell, Chad Hugo (fourth from right) and members of Spymob, after winning an award at the 2nd Annual Shortlist Music Awards Concert at Henry Fonda Theatre in Los Angeles, October 2002. L. COHEN/WIREIMAGE

Pharrell with Busta Rhymes and Justin Timberlake. DENISE TRUSCELLO/WIREIMAGE

Fuckin' posers: N.E.R.D (from left): Pharrell Williams, Shay Haley, and Chad Hugo, Chicago, August 30, 2002.

...had and Pharrell during a *Neptunes Present... Clones* album signing at Tower Records, Broadway and 4th Street, New York, August ?, 2003. JOHNNY NUNEZ/WIREIMAGE

...ccepting the Award for Producer of the Year, Non-Classical, ...the 46th Annual Grammy Awards, the Staples Center, Los ...ngeles, February 8, 2004. FRANK MICELOTTA/GETTY IMAGES

Pharrell with then-girlfriend Vashtie at the Sagamore Hotel in Miami, Florida. J. MERRITT/FILMMAGIC

Doobie brothers: Snoop Dogg and Pharrell onstage at the 32nd Annual American Music Awards, at the Shrine Auditorium in Los Angeles, November 14, 2004. FRANK MICELOTTA/GETTY IMAGES

Star Trak forever: leaving the Universal Music/Island Records aftershow party following the BRIT Awards, February 9, 2005. DAVID WESTING/GETTY IMAGES

arrell and Gwen Stefani have it like that at the 2005 American usic Awards, November 22, 2005. KEVIN WINTER/GETTY IMAGES

Wonderful place: with Mariah Carey for the 'Say Somethin'' video, on the Alexander III Bridge in Paris, France, March 09, 2006. MARC PIASECKI/FILMMAGIC

eet Yeezus! Kanye West and Pharrell at the Nokia Theatre in New York, August 29, 2006.
OTT GRIES/GETTY IMAGES FOR AMERICAN EXPRESS

He wants to move: on set for a video in Miami Beach, Florida, May 14, 2007.
GUSTAVO CABALLERO/GETTY IMAGES FOR THE CHAMBER GROUP

"No. I had to go."

Talk of politics led me to ask Pharrell whether, in the aftermath of 9/11 and subsequent invasion of Iraq, he was worried about the future? His reply was simple.

"The future is in our hands – we've got to do what we've got to do, and that's it."

Whose side was he on vis a vis the war?

"I'm not a political dude."

Did politics seep into his songs, however?

"Absolutely. There's a song called 'Drill Sgt' [on *Fly Or Die*]. Is it ambiguous? No, it's super-clear."

It was all a long way from high school in Virginia Beach where Williams was, he said with a smile, the class clown who talked too much in lessons. He only became popular towards the end of his time at school, by which point he had acquired an ability to empathise with life's downtrodden. He chose the name N★E★R★D as a statement of his understanding towards the dispossessed and disempowered. Describing his band as "backpackers in a world of drug pushers", he acknowledged that that didn't make them superior.

"We're not saying we're better. We're just saying that, in a world where vanity is glamorised and gluttony is glamorised… And we're part of it, actually!"

He suddenly remembered the subject of 'Provider', the track from *In Search Of…*, which was a true story about a drug-dealer friend.

"He turned his life around, and now he's managing one of our groups. He's not a hustler any more," he added, wistfully.

After a brief discussion of comic books, he told me that his uncle collected both DC and Marvel varieties. Williams then trotted out the now-familiar line about The Neptunes being Spiderman to N★E★R★D's Peter Parker.

Did he feel different as he undertook Neptunes and N★E★R★D projects?

"No and yes," he said. "No I don't feel different because it's still us, yes because of the differences of expression."

Were N★E★R★D, I wondered, more the "real" him?

"No," he decided, "it's the real us in both ways, but some things are for us and some are for other people." He added, somewhat inexplicably: "The real distinction is in what is intended..."

I told him how much I liked the new N★E★R★D single, 'She Wants To Move', and he seemed pleased.

"Wow," he beamed. "Thank you. Am I pleased with it? Yes."

This encouraged him to talk about several of the other tracks on *Fly Or Die*. There was one called 'Wonderful Place', which contained within it a hidden track entitled 'Waiting For You'. The former was melodic soft rock that recalled the mellifluous music of America's seventies FM radio, with an easy-going gait, a whistling refrain, and a jazzy inflection that recalled bands like Chicago. The latter was no less harmonically rich, semi-acoustic, with pizzicato strings, that seemed to be telling the tale of an abandoned child.

"It's pretty interesting," he said of the melodic structure, whose accessible charms belied the harshness of the message. "It's got different chord changes and cool melodies. Lyrically, it's basically talking about the aftermath of a nuclear war, but it's also about how the world is a wonderful place. It's cool."

There was another super-melodic double-whammy on the album – album closer 'Chariot Of Fire', which contained the grungier hidden gem 'Find My Way'.

"'Chariot Of Fire' is about a friend of ours, a fan, who had cancer," he divulged. "She's in remission now; she's our biggest fan."

The mooted second single, after 'She Wants To Move', was 'Breakout', an exquisite trifle with a jazzy break.

"I just like the way it feels," offered Pharrell, going on to explain that the song was about "a kid getting his ass beat and us just letting him know it's okay, you don't always win every battle in your life, sometimes you lose but you learn… acceptance."

Did he have a limitless supply of tunes in his brain?

"I don't know," he said, then paused to reflect on the question. "You'd better ask God that, because he made me."

Was the idea behind *Fly Or Die* to marry sweet music with lyrical content that erred towards the bitter?

"It's heavy lyrical subject matter but it's still delicate in what it's saying and delicate with the arrangements, with a lot of great chord structures," he explained. "We collected a lot and put them in the hamper and waited for this opportunity to use them."

Were Steely Dan an influence?

"No, not this time. It was more Afro-jazz, although the album doesn't actually sound anything like that in terms of influence."

With earlier tracks such as 'Provider' and 'Bobby James', from *In Search Of…*, and now 'Wonderful Place', were any subjects off-limits for being too dark?

"No. When you're writing you're not consciously making decisions as to what you are or what you aren't going to write. The music dictates the subject matter and the melody."

I wondered whether the artists he produced ever referred to specific N★E★R★D tracks and asked The Neptunes to "do one of those" for them? Did Britney Spears, for example, hear 'Bobby James' and ask for something similar?

"Sure," he said. "But you can't do it. Nah. You always gotta keep it fresh."

Was his ambition with Britney to be playful, even subversive, to deliberately alter people's perceptions of her?

"Nah, you just trust yourself and go in and the results dictate what it's going to be."

There was a knock at the hotel room door and Williams got up to answer it. When he returned to the couch I suggested that Kelis was The Neptunes' best fit, and compared it to other producer-artist relationships such as the one between Timbaland and Aaliyah, or even, going back a bit, the one between Burt Bacharach, Hal David and Dionne Warwick.

"All those guys were great," he said, his eyes lighting up at the references, but then he became distracted so I asked him what happened with Michael Jackson and the mooted collaboration with The Neptunes, the one circa Justin Timberlake's debut album that didn't quite come off.

"I talked to him but never worked with him," he recalled. "I met him several times and I talked to him. I met Michael twice."

What did he think of Jackson's behind-scenes problems and the speculation about his private life?

"I don't get involved," he replied, flatly. "I don't know much about it. I don't get involved in stuff like that."

As Williams' profile increased and his celebrity status, there would presumably be more speculation about his own private life. And yet, I suggested, he was in a better position than most because, as a producer, he could retreat into the studio?

"You're absolutely right," he said, delighted. "The funny thing is, I don't feel like a star. I got in this business to make good music. At the end of the day, you're right – the studio is my retreat."

Williams was now a feted writer, performer, producer, studio technician and entrepreneur – he wore a lot of hats. Which was he most comfortable doing?

"Making beats," he replied without hesitation.

How about his Billionaire Boys Club?

"The clothing line is more just me furthering my offer to the world as far as my perspective, that's all."

How did he define that perspective? He took the opportunity to expound a little on his fashion enterprise.

"It changes. It's seasonal. I collaborate with Nigo of [Japanese clothing company] A Bathing Ape and we've got the [Ice Cream] shoes coming in June."

Changing tack a little, I asked him – a decade before he would be elected as a judge on the US version of *The Voice* – whether he would like to be on the panel of *American Idol*?

"No," he replied, his rationale being that the existing judges already "do a good job", particularly Simon Cowell. Does he not find him too cruel to the contestants?

"No, I think he's hilarious to watch. He's really funny."

Was he worried about the future of the music industry, what with downloading and its impact on both the commercial and creative side of things?

"The world's gonna do what the world's gonna do," was his resigned reply. "You have to be comfortable with yourself and have the glory in your heart from what you do every day and not get caught up with those worldly things, as much as you can help it."

In Pharrell's eyes – or rather, ears – the young, rising English jazz-pop singer-songwriter Jamie Cullum was the future of the music industry. All day long he had been asking someone, anyone, from his entourage to get hold of Cullum's latest CD so that he could listen to it in the car.

"I asked for that shit hours ago, John!" he berated his then-press officer, John Coyne. "Now I gotta wait till later tonight. I'm not trying to be no asshole about that, but damn! I fuckin' admire this kid's work, man, and I gotta wait till later. It's pissing me off that I gotta wait this long to hear it. The kid's a genius. His tone, his interpretation through his fingers on the piano, is amazing. The kid's dope, man, he's a star. It's a shame the rest of the world don't know him, but things will change. He's incredible."

When was the last time he was this enthused about a new artist?

"It's been years. That's why I'm so excited. Only because his shit is so different – it's not hip hop, it's not R&B, it's something totally different."

Williams had evidently heard Cullum's early rendition of his track 'Frontin'', and it had blown his mind.

"Him singing my R&B-hip hop song through the interpretation of jazz was just so crazy – he had an upright bass instead of live bass or synth bass, a drum set – probably a three-piece with brushes – instead of programmed rhythms, and keyboards instead of my synthetic Rhodes... He played piano – that shit fucked me up. I plan to listen to this shit the whole time I'm here. I play it to death when I'm moved by music; I don't care about anything else."

Williams and Cullum would eventually collaborate in 2005, on an aborted track called 'Wifey', for Cullum's album *Catching Tales*. Meantime, I told Pharrell that there was a rumour going round that he was next going to be working with Jennifer Lopez (in 2003, The Neptunes had remixed 'Love Don't Cost A Thing' featuring Ghostface Killah, and they would meet again in 2009 when Williams produced and co-wrote her single 'Fresh Out The Oven', which she recorded under the alias Lola,. with US rapper Pitbull).

"Is that what they're saying?" he said, distractedly. "That's cool."

At that point, the phone in his hotel room rang, and he got up to answer. Then he fell back on the couch and returned to the matter at hand – J-Lo, and the prospect of a collaboration.

"I'm not at liberty to discuss who I'm gonna work with," he deflected, more gracefully than it appeared in print. "But I think she's interesting. She's talented."

Prolific and ubiquitous, did he ever worry that he would run out of songs? How did he keep coming up with new ideas?

"It's no different to how you conjure your questions," he mused. With difficulty, I joked. "It's not difficult. You're inspired by whatever. Like you might be inspired by the intrigue. Chasing the intrigue, you formulate your questions. And chasing the feeling I formulate my beats – no different."

How did he tap into the zeitgeist, song-wise, to come up with new ideas, new beats? With exotic substances or special exercise regimes?

"Nah. It's the same with asking questions – you do neither of those things."

I told Pharrell that I found tapping my head works and he laughed.

"That's probably a psychological... not blockage, no. You've probably just convinced yourself that that works. It's not real. Because when you tap your head like that there's no voices jumping in your brain. It's just what your mind has convinced you – it's just an illusion."

Did he never get writers' block?

"If I ever get writers' block, I'd write a song called 'Writers' Block'."

Did he mean that he tended to confront the problem head-on?

"That's right."

Had there been a moment in his career to date that he believed he would never beat?

"That happens every two or three years. Like, 'Oh my God, I can't believe I just did that!'"

Did he ever play his own tracks and think, "That's pretty damn good"?

"Not 'pretty damn good', but 'wow, that's emotional, I can feel that, that touches me, and I think this is gonna touch other people.'"

Ever industrious, Pharrell revealed that he was already working on new material, beyond *Fly Or Die*.

"I've got some new shit coming out, I can't wait for people to hear it," he said. "I purposely didn't do too much so that I could concentrate on *Fly Or Die*. I've got a barrage of things coming now. Production? Oh, come on. Beyond that."

Did he mean a solo album?

"Not solo, no. That won't happen yet."

Did ideas come out all the time?

"It's like conversation."

What were his favoured hours to work?

"From 2pm to 8pm."

Travelling all the time, did he write on tour by humming into his mobile phone?

"Yeah, I write in my phone. Then I sit at the piano."

He would even, he admitted, make use of pianos in hotel bars, for impromptu performances or writing sessions when the muse hit him.

As the first part of our formal interview came to an end, he explained that he played all the instruments on the first version of N★E★R★D's debut album, and on *Fly Or Die*, "We played from the ground up – but we've been playing since [Snoop Dogg's] 'Beautiful' and [Busta Rhymes'] 'Pass The Courvoisier'. And Justin Timberlake's songs were all live."

Did he still get a thrill hearing his own tunes on the radio?

"Absolutely. Still to this day."

Some time later, Williams, Shay, his brothers Pharaoh and David, plus his manager, his minder and his personal assistant were in the green room at Radio 1. Williams had gone there for an interview and a live session. He was waiting to record tracks for Jo Whiley's *Live Lounge* show with Spymob, his backing band, and to be interviewed by Radio 1 presenter Nemone Metaxas.

Meanwhile, he was transfixed by footage of riots showing on Sky News. The night before, an Aboriginal teenager had been impaled when he fell off his bike onto a metal fence, and Sydney police were blamed for chasing him.

"This is happening now?" he checked, his interest piqued. "A kid got impaled? Them niggas are snappin'. I'm gonna call Bono, write a song about it."

He slumped into a chair and began humming the melody to rock band Aerosmith's song 'Janie's Got a Gun'. There followed a 45-minute heated exchange between the musician and his entourage that appeared to be partly about who would or who wouldn't "bone a married woman" but mainly about a girl they all met the night before. Williams became quite animated, flapping his arms about and raising his normally gentle, mellifluous whisper of a voice.

He was still shouting as he was led off to record his *Live Lounge* performance.

"I do two things," he laughed, his voice trailing down the corridor. "I fumble, and I fuck. But I don't talk. You're a hater!"

Williams sustained the lively mood throughout the session with Spymob, three college rockers in standard-issue plaid shirts and woolly hats pulled tightly over straggly hair. "There are lots of white boys in here," he joked. "I call 'em my brothers. Can you dig it? Then you need a shovel."

Ever keen to move forward, he warned the technicians on the other side of the studio glass that he would not be performing anything from the last N★E★R★D album, *In Search Of...*.

"That's the old regiment," he chided. "Be adventurous."

Williams and Spymob ran through the latest N★E★R★D single, all jazzy chords and subtle shades of rhythm.

"'She Wants To Move'," Williams back-announced the track. "Probably because you have her chained down."

The BBC, he informed Radio 1's bemused staff, stood for Billionaire Boys Club. Then just as quickly Williams the cosmic hippie returned, all Curtis Mayfield-esque falsetto and ruminations on the "plastic" nature of reality, for N★E★R★D's 'The Way She Dance', which he explained was "about love at first sight – if that's ever possible".

"When your eyes are closed I hope I'm the man you see," he sang, although the mood was shattered somewhat by the line, "Big tits, fat ass, turquoise hair ..."

Finally, Williams the CEO offered shout-outs to his various sub-corporations and brand extensions. "N★E★R★D. Neptunes. Spymob. Star Trak. Billionaire Boys Club. Peace."

"I don't consider myself a pin-up," confessed Williams after the performance, in reflective, self-deprecating mode. "I'm not one of those dudes in magazines with insane muscles. If I was, I wish it would do me some good and get me a girlfriend."

This seemed a curious admission coming from one of the most eligible bachelors alive, although not as curious as his next pronouncement.

"I'd like to apologise to my future wife," he said, "but I've been busy doing the album for the people."

Outside, David Williams was enjoying some fresh British air. A furniture salesman from Delaware, he had joined his older and more photogenic brother for the European leg of this promotional tour. Pharrell, he revealed, hadn't changed much since becoming an international superstar.

It must be great, I ventured, being able to buy anything or do anything or go anywhere you want, whenever you want, and to be lauded wherever you go.

"People still have their demons," he said. "Money can't help that."

Did he keep his brother out of trouble on the road? "He don't get into trouble," he replied. "He keeps it simple."

Williams' busy schedule that day was due to continue with live and pre-recorded interviews at MTV in Camden, North London. In the car on the way to the TV studio he displayed an impressive recall of rap arcana.

"I grew up listening to that shit," he said, growing nostalgic. "I wish rap would go back to '88. 'The Symphony' [1988] with Marley Marl and Big Daddy Kane and Kool G Rap and Craig G and Masta Ace..."

What did he think of Grandmaster Flash?

"Still dope."

What, I wondered, was the song from the last 25 years that he wished he had written?

"Man... Lemme see..." There was a long pause as the car entered Covent Garden in Central London. Finally, he responded to the question.

"A song by Gil Scott-Heron called 'The Bottle' – that's crazy. Oh my God."

He started to sing the 1974 funk-soul classic addressing alcohol abuse, much loved by hip hop artists.

"'See that black boy over there runnin' scared/ His old man in a bottle...' That record was, 'Wooh!'"

I drew a comparison between Scott-Heron's bitter-sweet jazzy soul-pop, and the deceptively easy-on-the-ear music of N★E★R★D.

"He [Scott-Heron, who died in 2011] is so fuckin' dope, man," he gushed. "I'd love to meet him. All that Afro jazz shit was incredible. I'd love to bring that back."

Williams had worked with many stars, but would it be weird collaborating with his childhood heroes?

"Not weird. LL [Cool J, whom The Neptunes had produced in 2002 – the single 'Luv U Better' and attendant album *10*] is a fuckin' hero, man. He's dope. Chuck D [of Public Enemy],

Rakim – I'd be happier than a grizzly bear in front of 10 million picnics!"

Half an hour later, we had negotiated London's midday traffic and had arrived at MTV. There was a period of waiting, and so Williams passed the time slumped over a desk, complaining of backache. He was about to appear on a show about hip hop past and present, Pharrell's specialist subject.

"Talk to me about the Beastie Boys," demanded the presenter. Unfortunately, Williams wasn't in the mood now. In fact, he was shattered. Luckily, as Williams rested, Shay Haley was on hand to offer morsels of opinion on the subject. His contribution was to declare his amazement that white boys should have such incredible natural rhythm. Williams was gobsmacked.

"You sure you wanna say that?" he enquired of his N⋆E⋆R⋆D bandmate.

"I'm no racist," retorted Haley, somewhat hurt. "I love white girls."

Williams couldn't quite believe that remark, either.

"So did the [Black] Panthers," he said.

Trying to get the conversation back on track, the hapless presenter threw some more illustrious rap names at the pair. From this point, Haley decided, perhaps wisely, to keep quiet, and Williams finally decided to chime in, albeit tersely. Kanye West? "Dope." Missy Elliott? "She thinks outside the box. She's not afraid." Jay-Z? "A genius." Eminem? "Another genius." Tupac [Shakur]? "A soldier." Dr Dre? "Dre is Darth Vader. I'm just a Storm Trooper." The Neptunes? "That Pharrell," ventured Williams, throwing in a surreal non-sequitur to disarm the presenter and keep himself amused as his energies flagged, "has just started wearing boxers. I should know, cos I'm fucking his bitch."

There followed a 20-minute break between the programmes *Raw* and *TRL*, the latter a live MTV show that resembled a hip hop chart show aimed at the younger demographic, all whooping and hollering and nanosecond conversations between VJ and artist. Williams took the opportunity, before it started, to chat up female members of staff.

"Are you a sister?" he asked an Asian girl. "Whose sister?" she answered, quick as a flash. He playfully pinched her arm. She asked him to sign first a giant skateboard – an MTV competition prize – then a 12-inch single of 'Frontin''.

Williams' mood abruptly changed.

"You bring me one more thing to sign and I'm gonna..." he thought for a moment, "... tear it up and turn it into a paper aeroplane."

The woman from MTV seemed upset at this.

"You're rude," she told him. "You're so rude I'm going to tell the press how rude you are."

Williams didn't like the sound of this one little bit.

"If you do," he said, thinking aloud, "I will come to your house... and put your cat in a bag ... put in three mice ... and zip it up."

He looked pleased with this response. The young lady from MTV, on the other hand, seemed anything but.

"I don't have a cat," she said, disappearing with her clipboard.

With all promotion done for the day, it was time to pack up and head off for rehearsals for the next night's concert at the Hammersmith Apollo, the hottest gig ticket this season, which would see N*E*R*D joined onstage by Dizzee Rascal, Justin Timberlake, Black Eyed Peas and Gwen Stefani.

Williams' departure from the MTV building caused a veritable commotion, with something resembling Pharrellmania on the streets of north London. The police were forced to cordon off the area and there were females screaming from behind barricades.

"They sound like they're getting killed," remarked Williams, horrified but impressed. He ran over to sign autographs, only to find himself smothered by teenage limbs amid shrill cries of "Ohmygod!"

Even as the people-carrier glided smoothly through the crowd and down the street, Williams safely ensconced inside, fans continued to chase the vehicle.

"Look at these girls running," he grinned, pointing at one in particular. "Man, she's so cute." He made his PA, Stacy, open the car window to let her talk. The girl poked her head through.

"Hi, Pharrell," she gasped, breathlessly. "Star Trak for life!" He seemed touched by this.

"Star Trak for life, baby," he called back.

Was it like this everywhere he went?

"Yeah," he said. He could see one young lady going particularly enthusiastic in the crowd. "I feel like going over and saying, 'You want an autograph? Here you are, you deserve it, cos you're the loudest one.'"

Another female screamed, "Say hi to my cousin" and Williams shouted back, "All right!"

Did he really know her cousin?

"I think the girl that danced in the video to 'She Wants To Move' [British singer/entertainer Alesha Dixon, then of girl group Mis-Teeq] is her cousin. We don't know if it's true or not."

As the pandemonium receded, and back in the car, I asked Williams what it was like being mobbed, and he offered, modestly: "It's the music. It ain't me really."

What did the girls whisper to him when they hugged him.

"You know, the 'I love you' stuff: I love your music, I love you, marry me. All those flattering things," he revealed. He was nonplussed by his success, but eternally grateful for it. "Shit, I still ain't got over getting a Grammy [for the Neptunes –

producers of the year]. I'm afraid of getting over those things. To say, 'Yeah, I'm a Grammy award-winning guy.' I'm afraid to say that. I just think everything will come tumbling down after that."

Did his fame increasingly keep him from doing what he really wanted to do – the music?

"It's cool," he said, avoiding eye contact as the MPV silently passed through London at night, his face leaning towards the darkened window glass. "I have no complaints, man. Tired, but no complaints. I could be somewhere else, doing something I really don't want to do."

What would he have been had he not become an über-producer and celebrity studiocrat?

"I'd like to think I'd have become some sort of art teacher at least, or art professor at most, studying for my PhD," he considered. "But life doesn't always end up that way. Shit happens. I don't know what might have panned out."

Did he ever daydream about what might have been? "I would have been happy," he sighed. "I would have driven a Volvo and married another art teacher."

David Schwimmer, the actor who played Ross Geller in US sitcom *Friends*, declared at the time that he wanted to give up acting and become a lecturer. But surely, I argued, there can be no going back?

Williams wasn't convinced.

"When I find my wife," he said, "watch what I do."

He seemed to be suggesting that a life outside of music might have made him happier.

"No doubt there's a joy in sharing music with other people and seeing them at your show, agreeing with you," he said, looking out into the London night. "But the true glory is the element of discovery for yourself."

I asked him whether this had been a regular day in the life of Pharrell Williams.

"Every day is different, man. When it becomes routine, that's when I'll jack it in."

Were the reactions to him different in all the countries he visited?

"The people are all the same," he replied. "They've just got different names."

Finally, I wondered whether the perennially occupied Williams had a lot more lined up for 2004, or if he intended to take a break?

"I need to, but I'm not thinking about it," he said, somewhat vaguely. "I'm taking things one day at a time."

Paul Elliott of Q magazine met Pharrell in Ipanema Beach around the same time as I did and discovered someone who, as he wrote, "Thrives on confusion, always keeping people guessing about who the real Pharrell might be." He offered as some classic Williams contradictions the following: "He is the powerful mogul who still considers himself a fan of the artists he works with. The man who dreams of working with Michael Jackson when, realistically, Jacko should be begging him… An intelligent man who speaks of his fascination with nature while on Ipanema Beach and then heads to a nearby shopping mall to eat at McDonald's. A habitual flirt – no, make that walking erection – who insists he wants a wife. He has even written a song on the subject – 'Wifey, Where Are You?' – for Usher's new album."

Elliott found him guarded as an interviewee, which he attributed to tabloid exposés, circa 2002, concerning his supposed inability to keep up with Jade Jagger's sexual demands. That guard dropped just once during his time with Pharrell, when he wagered the price of a massage that he could obtain the phone number of a pretty shop assistant, and failed. Later, he caught sight of "a tall Demi Moore lookalike, her tight white trousers displaying a visible panty-line". He tutted: "I'm not mad at panties right now." Another girl caught his eye: "A pouting Latino beauty on a poster advertising sunglasses in a shop window," detailed Elliott. "That," offered Williams with a smile, "is my ideal girl: hot, but not perfect."

Whatever Pharrell was in search of, he still hadn't found it.

CHAPTER 6

Laugh About It

"It's totally weird to make Madonna sob, but even stranger when she tells everyone, 'Pharrell made me cry'"

–Pharrell Williams

In 2005, in an interview with *Scratch* magazine, the editors hailed The Neptunes as "modern Midases", the chart rulers who set the standard with regard to advances in production techniques and technology while managing to stay on top in terms of popularity. The magazine celebrated their simultaneous familiarity with rap's golden age and eighties pop, what it called their "space-age blend of classic pop and hip hop texture, strung together with a Zen-like ear for economical arrangement".

They were the sonic sorcerers without peer, with the possible exceptions of Timbaland, Dallas Austin, Dr Dre and Rodney "Darkchild" Jerkins, although when asked by Scratch who The Neptunes most admired and had most in common with, Pharrell Williams replied that it was Jay-Z.

"He really loves music and he's driven by the same thing we're driven by," he said, going on to name-check Puff Daddy as well. What set these people apart, he opined, was a determination not to repeat themselves, artistically.

"I'm interested in change, that's the only thing that will keep you here," he said, recalling some of his past highlights. "You can't do 'Slave 4 U again'. You can't do 'Grindin'' over again."

The magazine went on to elicit from the pair an example of what they considered to be classic pop and Chad Hugo replied: "A classic pop record is something from back in the day that you could play for kids today and they'd love it even if they never heard it before."

Pharrell had his own opinion on the subject, and was more specific. "To me, a classic pop record is classic because everyone loved it," he decided. "Pop was 'One More Night' by Phil Collins, it was [Michael Jackon's] 'Billie Jean', it was Madonna, it was Prince. It brought a sensation over the people."

He felt compelled to do his level best to ensure pop music was in as healthy a state as possible, adding that his job was "to conquer the beast – if pop sucks, change pop". And by "pop" he wasn't necessarily referring to the music's surface sheen but its potential to engage a wide cross-section of the buying public.

"I only call it pop because I think everybody will get it," he explained. "I don't call it pop because I think it's glossy or it has a certain kind of sound or whatever. I call it pop because I think it's gonna be popular."

What was remarkable about The Neptunes' brand of pop was that it managed to be progressive and popular – and it demanded a certain belief on the part of the musicians concerned that their way was the best way. This was, Pharrell acknowledged, how tracks as sonically far out as Clipse's 'Grindin'', and more recently Snoop Dogg's 'Drop It Like It's Hot', came into being – as a result of a certain openness towards unusual production, and an acceptance that the mainstream record-buying public have more of a penchant for radical sonics than they are often given credit for.

"There's only a few people willing or brave enough to go there," Pharrell ventured of The Neptunes' audacious production of Snoop Dogg's big hit from September 2004. He later explained to radio host Howard Stern that he wrote the chorus and his own verse while Snoop wrote his verses. Pharrell denied that the rapper was hard to work with.

"No," he said. "There are guys that totally get it. And they just never age because they get it. Snoop is one of those guys. Jay-Z is one of those guys. Some are more challenging because it takes them longer to get it."

Snoop evidently "got" 'Drop It Like It's Hot' from the word go. It featured a weirdly sparse arrangement, a loping beat and linear melody that seemed to only involve a single chord, plus assorted tongue clicks, white noise and a synth lifted from Danish electro group Laid Back's 1983 single 'White Horse' manipulated to sound as though it is repeating Snoop's name. Like Nelly's, 'Hot In Herre', Britney Spears' 'I'm A Slave 4 U' and Kelis' 'Milkshake' before it, and Gwen Stefani's 2005 single 'Hollaback Girl' after it, 'Drop It Like It's Hot' had a hook that, once heard, lodged itself in the listener's brain. It proved that number one hits don't have to be anodyne and bland, they can be forward-looking and experimentally funky.

"That was born out of a contact situation," Pharrell joked to Howard Stern when the infamous shock-jock asked him whether drugs were involved in the making of any of his records, specifically the Snoop one. "Whatever the aroma was, I wanted to stay under the [mixing] desk, for a while."

An intoxicating affair, 'Drop It Like It's Hot' didn't just prove popular, it stayed at pole position in the US *Billboard* Hot 100 for three weeks from December 11, 2004, making it Snoop Dogg's first number one on the chart – after 12 years in the game – with unarguably his most adventurous release to date. It was also his first Top 10 chart entry as a solo artist for a decade – since 1994's 'Gin And Juice' – gave him his first number one on the Hot R&B/Hip-Hop Songs chart, remained at the top for four consecutive weeks in New Zealand, and reached number 10 in the UK singles chart.

It fared almost as well critically. Wrote *Rolling Stone*: "The Neptunes' beat was light years from G-funk: a couple of tongue clicks, the odd drum machine hit and synth chord or two – the most deliciously minimalist music ever to slink its way to the top of the *Billboard* Hot 100."

It was nominated at the Grammy Awards of 2005 for Best Rap Song and Best Rap Performance by a Duo or Group, though it lost out on both counts to Kanye West's 'Jesus Walks' and The Black Eyed Peas' 'Let's Get It Started', respectively. The single was Pharrell Williams' biggest hit worldwide until 2013's 'Get Lucky' and 'Blurred Lines' (although his highest peaking single as lead artist is 'Happy'). On December 11, 2009, 'Drop It Like It's Hot' was named the most popular Rap Song of the decade by *Billboard*. Since its release the track has been certified double platinum by the RIAA.

If 'Drop It Like It's Hot' dominated 2004, 'Hollaback Girl' had a similar effect on 2005. Taken from Gwen Stefani's debut studio album, *Love. Angel. Music. Baby.*, it was the result of a determination on her part to add to pop's novelty pantheon: she actually conceived it as a latterday version of an eighties radio staple along the lines of Toni Basil's 'Mickey'.

"It was more about being able to indulge my theatrical, cheesy side and make something really fluffy, fun and light-hearted," she told the *Guardian* in 2007. "It was nothing to be taken too seriously, it was just a silly dance record."

That silly dance record, released as the album's third single on March 15, 2005, reached number one in Australia and the States, where it became the first digital download to sell one million copies – it later went on to sell a total of 1.2 million downloads and was certified five-times platinum by the Recording Industry Association of America. It was the fastest-rising single to reach the top in 2005, became Stefani's first US number one, where it remained for four weeks, and spent 31 weeks on the *Billboard* Hot 100, 29 of which were in the Top 50. On the 2005 year-end chart, the song was the second most successful single, beaten only by Mariah Carey's 'We Belong Together'. It also received several award nominations, including Best Female Pop Vocal Performance and Record of the Year at the 48th Grammy Awards.

It was reported that early attempts by Stefani and The Neptunes to create something of interest during the early stages of *Love. Angel. Music. Baby.* met with limited results, due to writer's block on her part. What reinvigorated her, towards the end of the sessions for her album, when she assumed she had enough material, was hearing tracks from Williams' own forthcoming solo debut, which made her envious, an underrated creative spur. So she decided to write another song with Williams, despite already having too many tracks.

"I was tired. I wanted to go home, but [Pharrell] was like, 'Don't leave yet,'" she recalled later. "So I come back, and he starts playing me his solo album. If something's really good, I get really jealous. So I'm like, 'You are a fricking genius. I can't believe I'm sitting in here with you right now, and you have these songs. We have to write another song.' I'm greedy," she added.

So the two started talking about what she considered the record to be missing, and they decided it needed an early riposte to fans of her band *No Doubt*. "I needed something about how they are probably like, 'Why is she doing this record? She's going to ruin everything,'" she explained. This spirit of preemptive antagonism became the genesis of the song.

Pharrell told Howard Stern that he and Stefani wrote it together in New York's Right Track studios in the early hours of the morning. They recorded as the sun came up and emerged, blinking, at 5 a.m. with the finished product. "It was awesome," he marvelled, casting back to his adolescence. "It was kind of, 'What can we do that is new, that nobody has seen before? I thought about high school, and the cheerleading squad. I thought about how the folks on the bleachers would play [Queen's] 'We Will Rock You'. So I thought, 'Let's take that sound of the bleachers…'"

To Stefani, it was an attitude-heavy "fuck-you" would-be anthem, written in response to a derogatory remark made about her by Kurt Cobain's widow, Courtney Love, in an interview with *Seventeen* magazine. Love had said, "Being famous is just like being in high school. But I'm not interested in being the cheerleader. I'm not interested in being Gwen Stefani. She's the cheerleader, and I'm out in the smoker shed."

Stefani, piqued by the idea that she might be regarded in such a conventional light, responded in the March 2005 issue of the *NME*, although she refused to name Love. "Y'know, someone one time called me a cheerleader, negatively, and I've never been a cheerleader. So I was, like, 'OK, fuck you. You want me to be a cheerleader? Well, I will be one then. And I'll rule the whole world, just you watch me.'"

A few months later, in *Rolling Stone*, she added: "I did the whole [album], but I knew I didn't have my attitude song – my 'this is my history, fuck you because you can't erase it' song. I knew I wanted a song like that."

Talking after it was recorded, Williams described Stefani as "like the girl in high school who just had her own style".

That style communicated itself successfully to most of the planet throughout 2005, helped by The Neptunes' brilliantly minimalist, audaciously sparse production, and a video set in high school, featuring Stefani, then 35-years-old, as a cheerleader. Its very ubiquity proved annoying to some: in an episode of satirical TV cartoon show *Family Guy* entitled 'Deep Throats', the canine character Brian watches a VH1 special on Gwen Stefani and declares, "I don't know what a 'Hollaback Girl' is, but I want her dead."

'Hollaback Girl' further claimed a space for Pharrell in the culture. It seemed appropriate, then, that later in 2005, Pharrell should appear on MTV with his own video diary, subtitled *The Revenge Of The N.E.R.D.* The intention was to show the experimental neophile "seek out new beats, new fashion, and boldly go where no artist has been before". The diary started at the beginning – with a trip back to Virginia Beach. Why? "Because every space traveller has to hold onto their roots." There was footage of Pharrell with his entourage driving around Virginia Beach listening to A Tribe Called Quest, the rap group who gave him the impetus to enter the music industry ("They're the reason I do music"). Dressed hardly incognito, in a Billionaire Boys Club baseball jacket and cap, he visited the local mall, the one where he used to go "to look for girls". He remembered going there growing up, just another anonymous teen; this time he was besieged by awestruck, tearful fans. He was mobbed everywhere he went, a veritable selfie-fest at every turn, with only his crew between him and a ravaging by the fame-hungry hordes, who he attempted to sate with autographs and photographs.

Pharrell was shown getting back into his limo and announcing that his next stop would be the airport, where he would be taking a private jet to Atlanta. The jet boasted its own bed. "It's actually nice," Pharrell admitted, "to enjoy the fruit of my labour." He said he thanked God a few times every day, "for bestowing the ability to conceptualise things and affect people with my music." He proceeded to ask: "What is my life without God?"

Once the jet landed, Pharrell was whisked off to a club, on arrival at which, surrounded as he was by a bevy of beautiful young females, he realised why the city was sometimes known as "Hotlanta". There were 5,000 women there to greet him, many of whom offered to buy the multimillionaire drinks. "I'm not looking out at how many girls are going to be into me," he told the adoring crowd. "I want to be into them."

He was stunned by the reaction to 'Drop It Like It's Hot', the crowd singing along with every word, even every nuanced beat. "I can't believe this is my life," he admitted to camera.

The final destination in his MTV tour diary was Japan, specifically Tokyo, where they had recently opened up a Far Eastern extension of his Ice Cream brand. He was delighted with the way the store looked. It was, he said with a delighted smile, "Far better than I ever imagined." He introduced Nigo, his collaborator and designer of the Ice Cream line.

While there, he took the opportunity to put on a special performance for all his "crazy, crazy" Japanese fans. "Japan is a kind culture," he noted with a laugh. "I'm always nodding my head and bowing."

Arriving at the venue, he was met with squeals of pleasure. "The Japanese love hip hop," he observed. He appeared on the balcony, like a royal dignitary, and did a Star Trak double-fingered V-sign to the audience below, to increased pandemonium. He remarked of the audience demographic: "It's a culture shock – there are no black people or white people." Then he realised: "[It's] the power of music. It transcends." A young local lady taught him how to say "bling-bling" in Japanese.

He concluded to camera, surveying the worshipful scene: "It's a good life, man. I never won the lottery, but I won this." Finally, an allusion to Charlie Bucket, the young hero of Roald Dahl's *Charlie And The Chocolate Factory*: "I've had the golden wrapper, man – I'm really that kid." And, he insisted, "It's all because of my fans." He acknowledged his adoring audience: "You have no idea how lucky you guys made me. I can't thank you enough."

As much fashion maven as R&B pioneer and pop idol, Pharrell was nevertheless bemused when magazines such as *GQ* and *Esquire* nominated him as Best Dressed Male. In 2005, he was caught leaning against a Bentley, in expensive haute couture, being shot by Terry Richardson, esteemed photographer to the stars, for an issue of the august journal. He found the experience surreal. "It's *GQ*, man," he said with an amazed sigh.

It was actually on the red carpet at the 2005 *GQ* awards that Pharrell made early mention of his debut solo album. "It's called *In My Mind* – I should be wrapping it up pretty soon," he said. He added: "It's a monster. It's going to eat away at the charts, and it's going to eat away at the girls' hearts." How do you do that, asked the interviewer? "I don't know," he said, momentarily baffled. "You just write from the heart and it just happens."

When, in 2003, Pharrell issued 'Frontin'', his debut single featuring Jay-Z, he insisted it was a one-off, that he was solely a producer and not an artist in his own right. And yet here he was, three years later, announcing the release of a solo studio album.

It had originally been scheduled for release on November 15, 2005, but it was delayed, Pharrell himself deciding it needed more work. "I was being super artistic, and I wasn't listening to anybody," he told *Billboard*. "I really didn't give [record company] Interscope a chance to catch up with me in terms of promotion." Nearly six months later, it was ready.

The Pop Matters website saw the delay ("Originally scheduled for release in 1948," it joked of the street-date shuffle) as a sign that *In My Mind* would be a sub-par piece of work. "When an artist pushes the release of his record back and back and back again, the implicit pre-verdict is that it's probably a steaming pile of monkey poop, or else it would have been natural and organic and expeditious and out already." This suspicion was confirmed when they heard the finished article. Despite the presence of three singles – 'Can I Have It Like That' (featuring Gwen Stefani), 'Angel' (only released in the UK and Europe) and 'Number One' (featuring Kanye West) – and cameos from Jay-Z, Nelly, Snoop Dogg, Kanye West and Pusha T of Clipse, Pop Matters found *In My Mind* "only so-so, offering a series of modestly tuneful, sometimes snoozy soul-pop-hip-hop songs".

Pitchfork weighed in, wondering aloud what would possess Pharrell to record his debut album minus the input of his longtime partner, Chad Hugo, who they decided was the John Oates to his Daryl Hall. "The dark curls and eccentric lazers… the evil synths and cold kinetics… in The Neptunes' music have always been attributed, at least in part, to Hugo," the site wrote in its review of *In My Mind*. Without Hugo's forensic touch Williams' music would be reduced to so much easy-listening R&B, which the site decided to term "yacht rap", an urban analogue to the more widely recognised yacht rock.

The AV Club identified the problem – it was, it surmised, inconsistency. "Inconsistency seems to be hard-wired into Pharrell Williams' musical DNA," it wrote. "With (and increasingly without) his Neptunes partner Chad Hugo, Williams has produced an astonishing number of perfect pop singles, from 'Grindin'' to 'Hot In Herre' to 'Drop It Like It's Hot'. But The Neptunes are also guilty of selling minor variations on the same forgettable beat to dozens of artists. As a solo artist, Williams suggests, at his best, a postmodern anime version of Curtis Mayfield. At worst, he sounds like a tone-deaf teenager warbling in the shower. Both Pharrells show up on *In My Mind*, his long-awaited, long-delayed solo debut."

Many of the reviews of *In My Mind* were negative, as though critics had decided that, after half a decade or more in the spotlight, hogging the charts, it was time to bring the new superstar of crossover rapped-up pop R&B down a peg or two. It wasn't so much that it was a bad album – although, regarding the lack of Hugo's maverick sonics and the occasionally hackneyed bragging in the lyrics, points taken – but rather that Williams had set such high standards with his collaborations, a stone-cold classic was what reviewers were expecting from his first bona fide solo foray.

Album opener 'Can I Have It Like That', featuring Stefani, was arresting enough. It started with a rattling barrage of beats and some brass, followed by an insinuating one-note bassline that provided the central motif. Pharrell was certainly in buoyant mood, referring to himself by his adolescent nickname of Skateboard P and hailing this, in the lyrics, as "the record of the year" before listing a few of the spoils of his labours, including his car and jet. 'How Does It Feel?' was a rousing seventies blaxploitation and psychedelic funk homage. 'Raspy Shit' – complete with four asterisks on the sleeve – was a funky midtempo affair bearing another reference to Skateboard P, as though Pharrell had intended him to be a character-motif running through the whole album. The chorus was sampled from his own verse on Snoop Dogg's 'Drop It Like It's Hot'. 'You Can Do It Too' was slow, jazzy, and appropriately featured jazz wunderkind Jamie Cullum towards the end. It caught Williams in a perhaps clumsily reflective mood: "My dick is being sucked down by a bitch called 'What now?'" he pondered of his easy-come success and uncertain future. 'Angel' was Prince-style falsetto funk. 'Young Girl', featuring Jay-Z, was better than the suspect title suggested. 'Take It Off (Dim The Lights)' was a fairly standard quiet storm slow jam, like an old Stevie Wonder ballad, one that you couldn't imagine Hugo allowing onto the album without messing with sonically in some way. 'Baby', featuring Nelly, was more interesting, rhythmically, even if the words again left a lot to be desired ("Meet me in the hallway where the bathrooms are," indeed). Worthy of a mid-eighties Michael Jackson groove, 'Number One' fared well on its release as a single, hardly surprising considering it featured the world's foremost producer and Williams' most likely successor, Kanye West.

Most reviews of the album agreed that the best track was 'Best Friend'. A rare autobiographical moment, it found Pharrell admitting, "I'm bottled up… I need a therapist," referring back to feelings of "doubt and defeat" as early as aged 10, reflecting on the death of his beloved grandmother, Loucelle, from leukaemia, and what may have become of him had he not met Chad Hugo. One of the recurring themes of his adult life to date was his inability to find someone with whom to settle down: "But I can't think of nobody I wanna share this with." By the song's middle, he was being exhorted to express himself ("Let it out, P, let it out"), lest his bottled-up feelings consumed him. 'Best Friend', according to *Billboard*, "Presents a glimpse of an alternate reality, of what Pharrell the MC could have become if he had been less focused on the spoils of fame and more adept at showcasing the backstory of his brilliant career."

Williams himself has tended to regard *In My Mind* as a false start with regard to his solo career. It was, he mused, the result of being inundated with riches and the trappings of success when his belief was always that money could never buy happiness: "Wealth is of the heart and mind, not of the pocket" as the rear sleeve of *In My Mind* proclaimed.

As he admitted in *GQ* in 2014, "I wrote those songs out of ego. Talking about the money I was making and the by-products of living that lifestyle. What was good about that? What'd you get out of it? There was no purpose. I was so under the wrong impression at that time.

"The money was too loud. The success was too much. The girls were too beautiful," Pharrell continued. "The jewelry was too shiny. The cars were too fast. The houses were too big. It's like not knowing how to swim and being thrown in the ocean for the first time. Everything is just too crazy. You're like, flailing and kicking and whatever, and you know what happens, don't you? You sink. My spirit sank. I just felt like, 'Fuck, what am I doing?'"

The problem, as he saw it, was a misplaced identification with two heroes: Jay-Z and Puff Daddy, two quite different artists. "So when I write a song on *In My Mind* called 'How Does It Feel'? – that's the one that goes: 'See me on the TV, the cuties they wanna fuck' – man, what was I talking about? That wasn't joy. That was just bragging. I wanted to be like Jay. I wanted to be like Puff. Those are their paths. I got my own path. But I didn't know what my path was. I knew that I was meant to do something different. I knew that I needed to inject purpose in my music. And I thought that was my path. I didn't realise that like, from 2008 up until now was, like, training. Like, keep putting purpose in everything you do. Don't worry about it; just put purpose in there."

Hindsight might have proven *In My Mind* to have been an ill-judged initial artistic salvo; nevertheless, it fared well commercially on its release in July 2006. It debuted at number three on the *Billboard* 200 chart and sold nearly 150,000 copies in its first week in the US, where it was nominated for a Best Rap Album award at the Grammys in 2007. Its lead single,

'Can I Have It Like That', peaked at number 49 on the US Hot 100 but went top three in the UK, where 'Angel', the second European single, reached number 15, and 'Number One', the third release, hit number one.

In 2007, Pharrell worked with Madonna, Beyoncé and Britney Spears. It was inevitable that he would eventually collaborate with Madonna, the Queen of Pop. It was for a song called 'Hey You', a charity record written by Madonna and co-produced by Pharrell, issued as part of the Live Earth environmental campaign, and made free to download from websites such as MSN. Twenty-five cents for each of the first one million downloads was donated to the Alliance for Climate Protection. It was Madonna's attempt at a global anthem, an 'Imagine' or 'Give Peace A Chance', although it didn't connect in such a major way with nations as did John Lennon's rallying cries for the human race did in the seventies and beyond. A stripped-down, folky ballad, it entered the lower reaches of the charts of a few countries including the UK, Canada, Sweden and Switzerland. She only performed it once, at the Live Earth concert on July 7, 2007, at London's Wembley Stadium, in an echo of 1985's Live AID extravaganza. There, she was joined by a choir of school children who provided backing vocals while Madonna sang against a backdrop of natural disasters and political leaders.

As for Williams, he performed at Live Earth, too, at the Brazilian leg in Rio de Janeiro. As his success grew, the demand for his involvement in charity events increased – the week before, on July 1, he performed at the Concert for Diana, in honour of the late Princess of Wales on what would have been her 46th birthday, also at Wembley Stadium. Broadcast in 140 countries across the world, with an estimated potential audience of 500 million, the event was hosted by Diana's sons, Princes William and Harry, who also helped to organise performances by many of the world's biggest stars. These included Elton John, Rod Stewart, Kanye West, Take That, Andrea Bocelli, Duran Duran and, of course, Pharrell, who performed Snoop Dogg's 'Drop It Like It's Hot' and N★E★R★D's 'She Wants To Move'.

Madonna, Diana... It had to be Beyoncé next, and it was: Williams and Chad Hugo produced a version of 'Diamonds Are A Girl's Best Friend', performed by Beyoncé for an Emporio Armani fragrance commercial. Directed by Jake Nava, responsible for many Beyoncé videos including 'Crazy In Love' and 'Single Ladies', it was a swish, stylish black and white affair just as striking as The Neptunes' production, which was an angular and minimalist take on the Jule Styne classic first performed by Marilyn Monroe in *Gentlemen Prefer Blondes*.

Towards the end of 2007, Britney Spears issued her fifth album, *Blackout*, featuring the Neptunes-produced 'Why Should I Be Sad' (aka 'Stupid Things'), with Pharrell on vocals, a multi-million-selling, high-charting (number two in the US and UK) testament to Spears' determination to continue making adventurous music that didn't recoil from confronting her troubled private life. Alexis Petridis of *The Guardian* remarked that, when faced with a public image in freefall, an artist has two options: making music "that harks back to your golden, pre-tailspin days" to "underline your complete normality" or "to throw caution to the wind: given your waning fortunes, what's the harm in taking a few musical risks?" Petridis commented that Spears opted for the latter and the results were "largely fantastic".

'Why Should I Be Sad' was produced and largely performed by Williams and Hugo and written by the former – apparently, Spears didn't ask for a writing credit. Still, it was as close as so-called synthetic bubblegum teen-pop gets to an autobiographical confessional, the lyrics addressing recent calamities in her car-crash of a celebrity life, particularly her relationship with her ex-husband

Kevin Federline. Full credit to Pharrell for managing to channel his inner Britney so sensitively.

It wasn't all girls and electronic dance-pop for Pharrell in 2007. That year, he went from *Blackout* to *The Black And White Album* by The Hives (there was also talk around this time suggesting that Williams was "very interested" in producing that other big alt rock band of the period, The Strokes, for their fourth album). The tracks that The Neptunes produced for the Swedish garage rockers' fourth album were 'Well All Right!' and 'We Rule The World (T.H.E.H.I.V.E.S.)', the latter released as a single. Several further tracks – including 'Windows' and 'Time For Some Action' – were recorded with The Hives but were shelved and later used for the long-awaited third N★E★R★D album, 2008's *Seeing Sounds*.

"He produced two songs on the record," said The Hives' frontman, Howlin' Pelle Almqvist, adding that "working with Pharrell was his idea". He explained: "We'd met him in 2004, and it was kind of too interesting not to do it. He doesn't really record rock bands that much, but that's what interested us in working with him. He's obviously a very talented guy who doesn't have all the same baggage rock producers bring with them into the studio. Working with him was way more spontaneous and more fun, I guess, because we didn't know what we were doing. It was fun for us to shoot from the hip."

There were variable amounts of fun during 2007 when The Neptunes worked with Madonna on her eleventh studio album, *Hard Candy*, released in April 2008. Williams and Hugo received a producer credit on seven of the 12 tracks, while Williams was credited with co-writing, with Madonna, the same seven songs. The remaining five were collaborations with Justin Timberlake and Tim "Timbaland" Mosley, with a cameo, and co-write, from Kanye West.

Having previously worked with relatively unknown producers such as William Orbit, Mirwais Ahmadzaï and Stuart Price, this time Madonna had chosen big-name artists in their own right. She justified her decision to MTV. "Because they're good, and I like their shit," she said, tersely. "I mean, I don't like to repeat myself, and I was sitting around thinking, 'What music do I love right now?' And it was actually [Timbaland and Timberlake's] record *FutureSex/LoveSounds*. I was listening to it obsessively."

The opening track on the album, Candy Shop, a metaphor for sex was the first team-up with The Neptunes. Williams described the scene as it was being put together. "We were just in a studio and Madonna was like, 'Look, give me some hot shit.' I was looking at her like, 'She's saying "hot shit"?' She was like, 'What?' And I'm like, 'OK.' So we just worked and made it."

The second track, and also the album's second single (following Timbaland/Timberlake collaboration '4 Minutes'), 'Give It 2 Me', was an urgent electro-dance tune and object lesson in success and survival ("Show me a record and I'll break it/I can go on and on") that didn't fare as well, commercially, as it deserved – it only charted on the *Billboard* Hot 100 for one week, reaching a peak of 57, although it did receive a Grammy nomination in 2009 in the Best Dance Recording category. Of the other Neptunes tracks, 'Heartbeat' was a synth-heavy affair, and 'She's Not Me' was disco revisited, with a Studio 54 bassline, choppy guitar motif worthy of Nile Rodgers, and Chic-style strings. Featuring a falsetto cameo from Pharrell, it was allegedly inspired by Madonna's then-husband Guy Ritchie. 'Incredible' was a typically off-kilter, rhythmically idiosyncratic Neptunes number. 'The Beat Goes On' also featured Pharrell on guest vocals and a rap interlude from Kanye West, and was like a Neptunes-enhanced 21st century take on the similarly titled 'And The Beat Goes On', the 1979 Solar Records monster dance hit for The Whispers. Finally, there was 'Spanish

Lesson', which was 'La Isla Bonita' revisited, all flamenco guitar and lyrics that appeared to have been cobbled together about a summer holiday romance, although as ever it was enlivened by The Neptunes' creative approach to beats. One couplet, however, seemed to be directed more at the producers than any fictional lover: "If you do your homework/Baby, I will give you more."

Reports that the making of *Hard Candy* was beset with creative tension rang true on the album's release: at times it sounded less like a Madonna album than a Timbaland/Neptunes one, with functional melodies and vocals on top.

Madonna discussed the album's making with Jonathan Moran of *The Sunday Telegraph*. "Just because you get a bunch of talented people together doesn't mean anything good is going to come out of it, so thank God it did," she said, a touch defensively. "I chose to work with Pharrell and Justin and Timbaland, knowing there was going to be a hip hop, R&B flavour to it, but hopefully I was going to put my spin on it as well."

She acknowledged that the experience had its challenges in the studio, not least because she was at the time the only one balancing parent-hood and a recording career. "They're very opinionated. They're all stars in their own right. Pharrell and Justin are also vocalists, singers. They do live performances and sing on their own records, and I don't usually work with producers and songwriters who sing themselves. They had very strong opinions about how I should sing things, and usually nobody tells me how they think I should sing something, do you know what I mean? So that was a challenge.

"Working with other strong-willed, strongly opinionated people is always a challenge," she continued. "You end up having to make compromises; sometimes people's feathers get ruffled. I said: 'Listen, all you guys, you don't have three children waiting for you at home like I do. I can't work till three o'clock in the morning.' So, once we got used to what everybody liked, we found a happy middle ground."

Not that happy. According to Pharrell, Madonna was something of a workhorse and disciplinarian. And there was so much tension and conflict between them in the studio that eventually Madonna was reduced to tears. "I totally made her cry like a baby. I had to get her a towel," he admitted to *Shortlist*. "We were alone recording the album and she kept talking a lot of rubbish, so I shouted a lot of rubbish and she started crying her eyes out."

Williams revealed that he had been unpleasant to Madonna, but said he had no plans to make their scrap public until the singer spoke about it herself. "I just said some really nasty stuff, I guess. And yeah, she cried for a really long time, actually," he said. "To be honest I can't believe she told someone about it. The whole situation was quite intense. It's totally weird to make Madonna sob, but even stranger when she tells everyone, 'Pharrell made me cry'."

Asked to elucidate by Howard Stern, who wondered whether Madonna resisted taking direction from her young producer, he replied: "Actually, Madonna did take direction. It's just that we had to box a little bit. We had a nice little scuffle. She said, 'You can't talk to me that way.'"

Pharrell couldn't remember her response, "but," he added, "the gist of it was, we kept doing this one take over and over and I saw she was beginning to get frustrated. I was trying to get her to deviate and try something different and she was like, 'I got it!' And I was, like, 'Okay.' And that kept happening and I was like, 'You can't keep talking to me that way.' And she was like, 'I'd like to speak to you upstairs.' So we went upstairs and had our little battle, and we hugged it out and it was cool."

Madonna's take on the incident, in an interview with *Nightline* in 2008, was as follows: "I was in a sensitive mood, I was singing and I didn't understand the rhythm that he wanted me to sing in, and he was kind of giving me a hard time and I was sort of taken aback by the way he was talking to me, so I said, 'You know what? We need to talk'. So we went upstairs and I'm like, 'You can't talk to me that way!' And then I just burst into tears and he was like, 'Oh my God, Madonna has a heart!', and I was like, 'What?!' and I started crying even more."

Still, there couldn't have been too many hard feelings, because Williams joined Madonna onstage for some performances on her Sticky & Sweet 2008-9 world tour. The reviews for *Hard Candy* veered between harsh and fair. *Rolling Stone* was surprised, as were many publications, that the queen of control allowed herself to be at the mercy of producers this time. "Dominance isn't just a fetish for Madonna, it's her religion. So it's surprising that her eleventh studio album is an act of submission – she lets top-shelf producers make her their plaything," it wrote, an opinion seconded by Stephen Thomas Erlewine from Allmusic, who felt that, "There's a palpable sense of disinterest [in *Hard Candy*], as if she just handed the reins over to Pharrell and Timberlake, trusting them to polish up this piece of stale candy. *Hard Candy* is that rare thing: a lifeless Madonna album." Ben Thompson of *The Observer* was more forgiving: "*Hard Candy* is a tough, nuggety confection offering plenty for listeners to get their teeth into," he wrote. "But it's hard to escape the sense that all concerned are going through the motions – effortlessly, sometimes brilliantly – but going through the motions, nonetheless."

There was nothing lacklustre about its chart performance: *Hard Candy* debuted at number one in 37 countries and was the eleventh best-selling album worldwide in 2008, shifting more than four million units. It became Madonna's seventh number one album, making her the female artist with the second most *Billboard* top-charting albums, behind only Barbra Streisand.

Typically productive, Williams also found time, in 2007-8, to record the third N★E★R★D album. Originally titled *N.3.R.D*, it was changed to *Seeing Sounds*, a reference to the neurological condition, synaesthesia, which means "sufferers" taste colours or, indeed, see sounds. "I think there's been a census done and they said, like, five percent of people in the world experience that condition and it's just basically when electrical impulses come from one of your senses and go to that receptor in the brain and go to other places as well," he told MTV. "For example, what you hear in your ear sends an electrical impulse to your ear, the auditory department of your brain, but sometimes it sends electrical impulses to other places like the visual part as well. That's why there are people who feel like they can picture smells or they can see sounds or hear a vision."

"I could always visualise what I was hearing... Yeah, it was always, like, weird colours," he told *Nightline*. He claimed with false modesty in *Psychology Today*: "I don't think I would have what some people would call talent and what I would call a gift. The ability to see and feel [this way] was a gift given to me that I did not have to have. And if it was taken from me suddenly I'm not sure that I could make music. I wouldn't be able to keep up with it. I wouldn't have a measure to understand." He admitted that he couldn't remember a time when he didn't associate music with colours that he visualised. "Oh my God, it's always been this way. But I thought all kids had mental, visual references for what they were hearing." He explained that synaesthesia was, for him, a pathway to writing music: "Sure, my lyrics are inspired by synaesthesia. You ask any great rapper or writer or musician, and they'll tell you their craziest ideas come from the shower or the plane because in both places there is sensory deprivation." He added that he believed one day people with synaesthesia would "rule the world" and listed some of the great "synaesthetes" of history, including Leonard Bernstein, Duke Ellington, Franz Liszt, Olivier Messiaen and Vladmir Nabokov.

Pharrell further explained that his intention with *Seeing Sounds* was to create music that would make sense in a live context. "Energy and emotion were the criteria, but we made the music anticipating the [live] show," said "third member" Shay Haley. "That was the most important thing."

And yet, it was hoped, *Seeing Sounds* would be sufficiently thought-provoking that people could enjoy it on their own: music to get lost in. Williams cited as an example one of the new tracks he'd written for the album, entitled 'Sooner Or Later', which he decided was "a great record to listen to and look at the clouds".

Haley further elaborated, vis à vis the album title, that N★E★R★D wanted to engender colourful sounds and auditory smells. On a simpler level, he wanted fans to "rock out" and be taken on an "emotional rollercoaster" by music designed to be blasted out of home or car speakers. As for Chad Hugo, he decided *Seeing Sounds* was a "big album of LSD, a sonic drug". All three described the record as an exercise in creative cohesion and band unity, which they approached with a renewed sense of purpose.

N★E★R★D funded the album themselves, and recorded it, with assistance on guitar and drums once more from Spymob, in two locations: the South Beach Studios in Miami, and the Record Plant Studios in Los Angeles.

Talking about some of the songs in detail on MTV, Pharrell described Spaz as "old school, hip hop feeling with some drum'n'bass. It becomes a big, tall monster. It's almost like this big gorilla looking down at you. If he smacks you, he kills you. His fingers are the size of your body. That's kinda what we're doing. We're facing this big monster of what we know is out there, of what we see, that big monster of energy". 'Everyone Nose (All

The Girls Standing In The Line For The Bathroom)' was, he said, "just like a schizophrenic musical pillage to the ears".

In terms of musical styles, *Seeing Sounds* would comprise a barrage, rather than a blend, of hard rock, funk and soul, much like *In Search Of....* Hugo described it in terms of a return to the band's roots: classic rock with a seventies funk swing.

"We don't care about genres," declared Williams. "We're not doing this for the money. We're doing this for people who pledge allegiance to our movement."

Added Hugo: "We just want to make people move."

What was important, they stressed, was bringing energy back to music – they cited Limp Bizkit's 1999 single 'Nookie', and the most recent album by Red Hot Chili Peppers, 2006's *Stadium Arcadium*, as the last truly impressive high-energy records.

"That," offered Haley of the Chili Peppers album, "had a few joints up there that commanded you to go berserk and just mosh or punch the closest person to you in the face."

The aim, according to Williams, was to achieve the clarity and impact of an old Beatles album. "I said to Andrew [Coleman, N★E★R★D's engineer], 'You've heard those Beatles records. Let's put the drums and bass on the right, keys in the middle, and the mothafucking guitar and backgrounds on the left. Let's go!'"

To assist in the creation of this vaunted high-energy, impactful sound, N★E★R★D drafted in members of The Hives – Chris Dangerous (drums/percussion), Nicholaus Arson (guitar), Vigilante Carlstroem (guitar), Dr. Matt Destruction (bass) – who played on 'Time For Some Action' and 'Windows', with their frontman Howlin' Pelle Almqvist providing guest vocals on 'Time For Some Action'.

On its release in June 2008, *Seeing Sounds* debuted at number seven on the US *Billboard* 200 chart, selling 80,000 copies in its first week, and peaked in the Top 20 in Australia, Canada, the

Netherlands, Switzerland and the UK. The first single from the album, 'Everyone Nose (All The Girls Standing In The Line For The Bathroom)', was a Williams/Hugo composition and production about women snorting cocaine in lavatories, apparently a new trend observed by Williams on his tour of the world's clubs.

"Yes, when the girls go in the bathroom, they're powdering their faces with that other white stuff," he explained. It reached number 17 in Japan and number 41 in the UK. The second and final single lifted off *Seeing Sounds* was 'Spaz', which only managed to reach number six on the US *Billboard* Bubbling Under Hot 100 chart, although it did get used in a TV commercial for the Microsoft Zune.

Still, reviews of the album were favourable enough. Some critics deemed it N★E★R★D's best album to date. Anthony Henriques of PopMatters praised the production, saying that "their signature drums and spaced-out samples sound as good as ever here", adding that "the overall balance between live and electronic instrumentation is also the best they have managed on any of the N★E★R★D albums". Christian Hoard of *Rolling Stone* felt that the album was "experimental and expansive" while Sal Cinquemani of *Slant* magazine hailed its "freshness or spontaneity" and Priya Elan of *The Times*, in a four-out-of-five-star review, decided the band were "pushing the boundaries of the popular song".

There were some negative notes struck, for example by Alexis Petridis of *The Guardian* who pointed out that the songs were "largely about sex", calling said approach "wearisome", and Ian Cohen of Pitchfork called the album a "baffling, obnoxious mess". But N★E★R★D's third album was largely welcomed. As were the band's concert dates. From April to June 2008, they toured with Kanye West as an opening act along with Rihanna and Lupe Fiasco as part of the Glow In The Dark Tour. On June 13, they appeared at the Isle Of Wight festival. In a nighttime set including

'Rock Star', 'Lap Dance', 'Fly Or Die',' Everyone Nose' and 'She Wants To Move', they wowed the crowd. "If you've come here to party say 'hell yeah!'" yelled Pharrell after playing 'Backseat Love'. Hugo added: "It's a privilege to be rockin' out with all you guys," before the band played 'Rockstar', eliciting unison bouncing and dancing. "I wanna fuck tonight," declared Williams during a frenetic rendition of 'She Wants To Move', prompting an X-rated crowd sing-a-long. At the climax of the set the band sampled 'Seven Nation Army' by The White Stripes, rapping over the guitar riffs. The band startled all-comers by leaping into the audience and mingling with front-row fans.

On *Seeing Sounds* tracks such as 'Laugh About It' N*E*R*D found the perfect middle ground between the stun of hard rock, the swing of jazz and funk's rhythmic imperative. When the band ended the year with a sold-out performance at the House Of Blues in Chicago, with special guests Bad Brains, the eighties hardcore punks, and then toured with nu metal outfit Linkin Park, it made perfect sense. Because if there was a single musician in the noughties who merited the description, "all things to all people", it was Pharrell Williams.

CHAPTER 7

Busy Doing Nothing

"We just want to do something different; we want to change the world"
— Pharrell Williams

It would be easy to assume that, compared to his current ubiquity, post-'Get Lucky', 'Blurred Lines' and 'Happy', Pharrell spent the late noughties and early 2010s relatively under the radar. The truth is, there wasn't a time when he wasn't working, and virtually everything he did was high-profile, even if his collaborations during this period weren't quite as stratospherically successful as his 2012-14 output. He might not have been as chart-ubiquitous as three or four years earlier, and N★E★R★D had arguably yet to match critical regard with commercial fortune, but still he kept working, like a man on a mission. Happiness, according to Pharrell Williams, is a job that engages you so fully that you actively pursue being a workaholic.

As he said in 2009, pondering the alternative, which as he saw it was a life of meaningless pleasure-seeking, "The only thing that suffers is your social life, but what is that?"

In 2009, he collaborated with Colombian artist Shakira on four tracks from her eighth studio album, *She Wolf* – 'Why Wait', 'Good Stuff', 'Long Time' and 'Did It Again'. The latter, an electro-R&B number with a samba inflection seemingly concerning infidelity, was released as the second single from the album. It went Top 20 in Spain and Italy and reached number one on the US *Billboard* Hot Dance Club Songs chart.

The same year, Pharrell also worked with another Latina dance star in need of a career injection: Jennifer Lopez aka J-Lo, who decided to reinvent herself once again, for *Love?*, her seventh studio album, recorded using the pseudonym Lola, perhaps under the influence of Beyoncé as Sasha Fierce. The track that The Neptunes co-wrote (with Amanda Ghost) and produced for her was 'Fresh Out The Oven' and featured another Latino, rapper Pitbull. Although dismissed by Digital Spy as "a pretty standard sexy electro-R&B jam", like Shakira's Pharrell team-up it reached pole position on the Hot Dance Club Songs chart.

Another Hot Dance Club Songs chart-topper was The Neptunes' remix of Michael Jackson's (actually The Jackson 5's) 'Never Can Say Goodbye' from a 2009 album entitled *The Remix Suite*. This was a compilation of remixed Jackson 5 hits largely synonymous with Michael, issued in the wake of the superstar's death earlier that year. The credits read like a who's-who of the period's stellar producers, and included such luminaries as Dallas Austin, Stargate, Benny Blanco, Salaam Remi and the late Frankie Knuckles. Williams' and Hugo's interpretation of the 1971 single was distinctly Neptunes-flavoured and featured Pharrell declaring, towards the end of the song: "This is my mom's favourite record. I hope you don't mind me doing this."

"We jumped at the opportunity to be involved with this project because Michael is a legend who influenced our entire career and redefined the world of music," Pharrell said at the time, and even if The Neptunes' proper full-scale collaboration with Jackson would now never happen, this did at least provide them with an opportunity to pay homage of sorts.

The Neptunes didn't just work with household names, however. In fact, they had a history of producing relative unknowns and offering a helping hand to rising talent, including Boo Bonic, Chester French, Kenna, Kid Cudi and Malik Yusef. And 2009 was no exception, because that year Pharrell made a guest appearance on, and co-wrote, 'ADD SUV', a song by French indie-electro artist Anna-Catherine Hartley alias Uffie. She said she always knew her song mocking her generation's obsession with material possessions, especially cars, would feature Pharrell.

"I was so excited when I was introduced to him in Tokyo a few years back that I knew if there was ever the right track I would have to ask him to be on it. This was that track and, fortunately, he said 'yes'," she said, beaming, although to prove that even Pharrell's stellar name was no guarantee of success, the single stalled at number 28 in the UK Independent Singles chart and number 31 in the UK Dance Singles chart.

Right at the other end of the fame spectrum was Jay-Z whose 2009 album, *The Blueprint 3,* was a showcase for the biggest producers of the day: Kanye West, Timbaland, Swizz Beatz. There were also rapping and singing cameos from everyone from Drake and Rihanna to Alicia Keys. It was probably inevitable, then, that Pharrell would be invited to make an appearance on Hova's eleventh studio album, on a track entitled 'So Ambitious'. Based on a sample of a song called 'Memory Lane' by Minnie Riperton, it almost didn't make the cut – apparently Pharrell emailed Jay-Z the track on the day he was mastering the album and he loved it so much he instantly paused, so that he could accommodate this eleventh-hour marvel. 'So Ambitious' was aimed at parents who attempt to limit the dreams of their children – it was a song apparently borne of bitter experience for Jay-Z and Pharrell.

"We wanted to make a record that speaks to kids. There's a couple of lewd words there, but I wanted to make sure that kids heard this record and felt inspired," Williams told MTV News. "That's why there's a little bit of anger to it. There's anger in his verses, there's anger in my chorus. That's why I say spiteful things at the top [of the record]. There's anger there, because there's heat. Because you're young and people are telling you what you can and can't do. Unacceptable."

The producer and the rapper had had their fair share of successful collaborations in the past, from 'Frontin'' to 'I Just Wanna Love U (Give It 2 Me)', but this was the first time they had recorded a track where they weren't together in the studio: 'So Ambitious' was completed while they were in different locations.

"We did it all by phone," Williams explained, swept away by the celestial beauty of the backing track. "One-hundred percent. Phone and e-mail. I've never done that before in my life. I just sent him the joint, 'cause he beat me up for the whole album. He was just kinda like, 'I need something to really tell a story.' And I was like, 'OK.' And I sent him this track. I said, 'I'm sending you clouds with 808s [drums] under it. There's just clouds, and it's expansive. You can just speak. It's a blank canvas.' Then I sent him the hook and played it for him, and he lost his mind.

"Just the attack on it," he gasped of the song. "Ferocious."

Jay-Z wasn't the only rapper treated to Pharrell's studio magic in 2009. He worked with Jayceon Terrell Taylor, better known as Game, on his fourth studio album, *The R.E.D. Album*. (It wasn't actually released until 2011, after nearly a dozen attempts to reschedule.) Williams is credited as executive producer although he only received a co-writing credit on one of the tracks, 'Mama

Knows' featuring Nelly Furtado. The Neptunes were also two of 15 producers listed on the credits of Snoop Dogg's tenth album, *Malice In Wonderland*, which reached number two in America's Top Rap Albums chart, although again they only actually produced one of the tracks, 'Special', which also featured Pharrell and R&B singer Brandy.

Meanwhile, N★E★R★D went on the road. In 2009, Pharrell looked back on the genesis of the band with hiphopnews24-7.com and described it as "ethereal music designed to take you somewhere emotionally". What was missing, he said, was the energy that would translate that music to a festival crowd. "So we went back in the studio with Spymob from Minnesota," he said, reminiscing about the moment that *In Search Of...* Mk 1 got remade/remodelled and, in the process, became more of a live statement declaring their "authentic" rockin' credentials. "And that's where it started, and we played 'Rockstar' and it felt incredible, and we never looked back. Now we're approaching our fourth album."

As the website n-e-r-d.com explained, extolling the virtues of this hard-gigging band, "This is a band that still grinds it out as if they were a starving local band working the club circuit. Two-thirds of their year is spent on the road, touring incessantly. They play big metropolises and small Midwestern cities, from festival shows to more intimate college campuses. Certainly, it's not something they would ever have to do. But it's in the experience of playing live, in creating and sustaining and riding that connection with their audience, that they discovered the essence of their music and for why they exist."

Pharrell saw the stage as the site for trying out new music and making a connection with his audience."If you want to know how to run something, you gotta work in the mailroom first," he ventured. "Playing live is our mailroom, it's our laboratory, it's where you see the connection between music and your songs and the fans and the reaction you get all in one place."

For Shay Haley, nothing could beat the thrill of a positive crowd reaction to their music. "There's no greater feeling than looking out at an audience, whether it's in New York, Australia or Japan, and seeing kids – black, white, Latino, male, female, whatever – shouting the words back to you or rockin' out and having a good time," he said. "It is the most beautiful thing."

In July 2009, N★E★R★D performed on the Pyramid Stage at the Glastonbury Festival. It wasn't quite as full a set as Pharrell might have liked, however; because they were around 25 minutes late starting their performance due to technical issues, the sound was pulled on them shortly after starting 'Everyone Nose (All The Girls Standing In The Line For The Bathroom)', which proved to be the final song in a nine-song set. He invited fans to dance with him onstage during penultimate track 'Lapdance' and shouted at the festival organisers. "We came all the way from the USA to play for 200,000 people," he screamed. "Quit saying I've got five more minutes!"

He paid tribute to Michael Jackson, who died a month earlier, declaring, "R.I.P. Michael Jackson!" during 'Sooner Or Later'.

Pharrell managed to keep his cool during a filmed interview at Art Basel in Switzerland, the self-styled "world's premier international art show for modern and contemporary works". He was there to discuss his collaboration with artist Takashi Murakami and jewellery house Jacob & Co. and their creation, The Simple Things. This comprised a cupcake, a bag of Doritos, a bottle of Heinz ketchup, a Pepsi can, a sneaker, a condom, and a bottle of Johnson's Baby Lotion – all encrusted with 26,000 rubies, sapphires, emeralds, and diamonds inside the mouth of a Murakami sculpture.

The interviewer asked whether he released endorphins when he created. Immaculately, snappily attired in a brown hat, red check shirt and blue overcoat – the last word in cool, chic style – Pharrell replied: "I'm a musician by trade. I'm a fortunate guy who's been given the opportunity to express myself... I consider myself blessed. Just happy and excited to be in the position I'm in." She asked if he was wearing "bling" and he retorted, curtly: "Bling I do not wear. I'm not a rapper, so... I rap here and there but that's not my day job. My day job is as a producer, and 'bling' is a term that was given to a certain type of rap artist. I wouldn't categorise myself as that. In terms of diamonds, yes, I do wear diamonds. But it doesn't define me, nor is it something I can take with me when I pass."

In 2010, N★E★R★D supported Blur frontman Damon Albarn's extracurricular project Gorillaz on their Escape To Plastic Beach World Tour. During the tour, Albarn recorded a song with Williams but it was not featured on Gorillaz' fourth album, *The Fall*. Also unreleased were tracks recorded with Christina Aguilera, Canadian rapper Drake (a number provisionally titled 'Dirty Looks') and controversial cartoonish hip hop-R&B diva Nicki Minaj. A further sign of Pharrell's versatility came when he composed the soundtrack – the score and incidental music, as well as a slew of bespoke songs such as 'My Life', 'Fun Fun Fun' and 'Prettiest Girls' – for the animated comedy *Despicable Me*; it was produced by Hans Zimmer and recorded with the Hollywood Studio Symphony.

And in a year in which The Neptunes produced, among many others, Kelly Clarkson, Lupe Fiasco, Nelly, Swedish House Mafia, T.I., Gucci Mane, Ciara and CeeLo Green, there was a further sign of Pharrell's prolificacy when, in October 2010, fairly hot on the heels of *Seeing Sounds*, N★E★R★D issued their fourth album, *Nothing*, through their Star Trak imprint.

Pharrell warned fans to expect "a departure" this time, and an album more serious in tone. Earlier in the year, he had spoken about the need to "do things that are unconventional. I think I want to broaden the N★E★R★D brand and expand it in a way people are not necessarily expecting. It's time for N★E★R★D to spread its wings and reinvent the definition of the experience of N★E★R★D, and that will be happening very soon."

In an interview with billboard.com about the new album, he said the plan was to make a "timeless album that's kind of a time capsule, so 10 years from now people look at that album and go, 'I remember that era. That's when the *Nothing* album came out.' I just wanted to make some good music that would affect people in a good way."

Not that *Nothing* came particularly easily. In fact, there were delays and as many as 27 tracks were scrapped because Williams, ever the perfectionist, "didn't feel like we were pushing ourselves as much as we could. We needed to perfect the sound, so we kept pushing the date back until it was right. When we looked back on those [27] records, they weren't really saying what we wanted to say. They weren't good enough."

"It didn't feel right," Shay Haley continued, rationalising the decision to shelve a year's worth of studio graft. "Sitting there and listening to it, it was definitely a new sound, an experimental sound. With a little bit more work, we'd have had something that the average person probably would've been just as happy with. But we would know. Our core fans would know. It wouldn't be us."

"I believe in making 'something' out of 'nothing'," added Chad Hugo. "Anyone who makes art or expresses themselves in any creative way, it's a challenge to empty out the cup and then try and refill it again. You want that challenge, to see if you can come up with something new and not rely on what you've done before. That's how we motivate ourselves."

One of the main inspirations for the new album was, decided Pharrell, womankind: *Nothing* would be geared towards females.

"This album, I think, is made for the women who like to take a load off and feel," he said. "This album is all about feeling. We made the first three albums, and there was a lot of thought put into it. But this album, I feel we put a lot more feeling into it. There is thought, but there's more feeling… I feel like we did what we set out to do on the first album, which is to have a lot of fun and give people music that they could feel, because I feel music is in a wonderful place right now. It's changing – it's feel-good music – there's also the wars and I just think people are tired of thinking about that type of stuff all day long and they just want to go back to feeling so they can remember who they are. But we just want to talk to the girls…"

Contradicting this idea of *Nothing* as escapist entertainment, in an interview with billboard.com he explained that *Nothing* would be an album where N★E★R★D reflected serious contemporary issues.

"We needed to align ourselves and make ourselves parallel and congruent with what society is feeling," he said. "People are concerned with war and the world. People are still dealing with their issues even if we think things have changed. We wanted to go back to talking about whatever we feel, whatever we saw. When we first started playing music, we started with nothing and that was a pretty cool place to go back to."

There were certainly a fair share of tracks on *Nothing* that could be filed under "topical" or that concerned social issues, from 'Help Me' which addressed the military-industrial complex ("the war machine", as Pharrell sang in his gently insinuating falsetto) to the eco-conscious 'Life As A Fish' and 'God Bless Us All', which Williams explained was "about a friend of ours in the business, a superstar who went through a crazy, rough patch and we wanted to offer him words of encouragement."

According to Pharrell, *Nothing* was a response to the changing times. "The world is crazy," he declared. "We're on our little hippy kick. Thank God we caught it."

Asked whether his "hippy kick" represented a reprise of late-sixties and early-seventies values, he replied: "I don't know if we're making any statements. We think the way to promote change is working on yourself, one person at a time, and I think if we can inspire you and encourage you to be ambitious, then you have become aligned and you are one of, I don't know, six billion people on the planet. That's all we're trying to move: one person at a time." His ambitions, he insisted, were modest. "We just want to do something different; we want to change the world."

With such hippyish talk, it made sense that the music would also evoke that late-sixties and early-seventies moment, and sure enough, the influences on N*E*R*D this time apparently included such behemoths of rock as America, Crosby, Stills & Nash, Moody Blues and Creedence Clearwater Revival. As Shay Haley put it, if *In Search Of...* drew inspiration from the likes of Earth, Wind & Fire and Steely Dan, then *Nothing* was "more like The Doors or the band America."

Pharrell acknowledged the impact that working on the *Despicable Me* soundtrack had on him, because that, too, led him back to the sixties. "It really helped me for *Nothing*," he said. "It prompted me because of the learning experience I got working at Hans Zimmer's compound. It was pretty amazing! There were so many sounds and so many different directions. It was just really interesting... I'd probably compare it to a Quentin Tarantino soundtrack – probably *Reservoir Dogs*. You've just got to hear it, man. It's in the spirit of the late sixties/early seventies. You know, revolution! It's definitely the next step up from *Seeing Sounds*."

He told *Clash* magazine that he believed the songs on *Nothing* were N*E*R*D's most instantly enjoyable to date. And certainly that idea was borne out by album opener 'Party People', a catchy, insistent blast of electro-funk that featured a brief cameo from rapper T.I. "Let's just go!" shouted Pharrell, and it was hard to refuse.

'Hypnotize U', the second track, was the next to be lifted off the album for single release in October 2010, when it was accompanied by a video in which a gaggle of beautiful women were in hypnotic thrall to Pharrell. The track featured his best Prince-ish falsetto, which was a heavenly approximation to some ears, an aberration to others. It was produced by Daft Punk, the first collaboration between The Neptunes and the French robo-funkers since the former's remix of the latter's 'Harder, Better, Faster, Stronger' in 2001. It was a last-minute, unexpected exercise.

"I bumped into those guys and we hadn't worked together in almost 10 years," said Pharrell, "so we decided to do something together and it was super cool, like a magical moment out of nowhere happening in the fourth quarter."

'Help Me' (accompanied by a viral video which could be seen on the Billionaire Boys Club/Ice Cream website, ditto 'Life As A Fish') was a woozy, swaying number that burst into a brass section more than vaguely reminiscent of producer Paul A Rothschild's horn charts for The Doors circa *The Soft Parade*. 'Victory' was slower, torpid funk-rock that recalled Lenny Kravitz and featured background vocals from Rhea Dummett, who would later sing on Pharrell's global hit single 'Happy'. 'Perfect Defect', reminiscent of a funky Steely Dan, was the start of a diaphanous, jazzily melodic album midsection. 'I've Seen The Light' (with more Rhea Dummett background vocals) was slow celestial funk with harmonies and an exquisite "hidden" interlude called 'Inside Of Clouds', famously sampled later that year by Pharrell acolyte Tyler, the Creator of notorious LA rap crew Odd Future. 'God Bless Us All' was a jazzy doodle marked by horn blasts. 'Life As A Fish' (again featuring Rhea Dummett) was otherworldly, heady, swirling, cloudy R&B with ethereal lyrics that intimated, perhaps unfairly, that Pharrell had just two lyrical modes: spaced-out and sexed-up. The lustrous chord sequence recalled Bobby James from *In Search Of...* while the lyrics ("Stop sending your trash to sea") assumed an aquatic point of view. Well, Brian Wilson of The Beach Boys did once sing a song from the vantage point of a tree…

Closing the "redux" version of the album were the choppily rhythmic digital funk of 'Nothing On You', which drew comparisons with Justin Timberlake's *Justified* album and could have been released as a single, and 'Hot-n-Fun', which gave the lie to the theory that *Nothing* was all politics and no fun. An utterly irresistible funk charge featuring R&B songbird Nelly Furtado, it was issued as the album's lead single earlier in the year, when it became a Top 30 hit in Italy and Belgium and a number one on the US Hot Dance Club Songs and UK R&B Chart.

The deluxe version of *Nothing* added four tracks: 'It's In The Air' – prefaced by a snippet of vituperative invective from March 2010, of Democrat (and Kennedy family member) Patrick Kennedy – was the most overtly political track on the album, with a jazzy swing like something from the pre-rock era. 'Sacred Temple' had the dynamics and surging power of classic rock, only with an R&B bassline. 'I Wanna Jam' was classic rock in excelsis, recalling Spirit's version of Jimi Hendrix's version of Bob Dylan's 'All Along The Watchtower', with a chorus that was pure teen anthem, with a typically priapic lyric ("life makes me horny"). Finally, 'The Man' was slower, more Neptunes than N★E★R★D, featuring a chorus ("Don't it feel good") that sounded more like a question than an affirmation, with whinnying sounds, the whistling refrain from classic spaghetti western *The Good, The Bad & The Ugly*, and shouts of "Revolution!" and "Liberation!" from Pharrell.

If the messages on *Nothing* were simplistic or vague, the music was dense with allusions, confirming the band's rampant eclecticism. And, notwithstanding 'The Man', so different to The Neptunes that it suggested this was one of the few occasions in pop history when the same musicians had carved out two separate demographic niches among their potential audience.

Although the music on *Nothing* was largely credited to Williams and Hugo (unlike the Williams-heavy credits for *Seeing Sounds*), the front cover of *Nothing* showed Williams by himself, in profile, wearing a military helmet, bearing red, white and blue feathers. Still, if this was a militant, patriotic Pharrell, the contents of the album didn't quite bear this out, but certainly it was the most enjoyable N★E★R★D album since *Fly Or Die*.

Its release in November 2010 confirmed that, whereas The Neptunes sold records in vast quantities to a massive and mainstream dance/club/R&B audience, N★E★R★D's fanbase was rather more selective, their appeal on the cult side, a strange thing to say about a band comprising, as its frontman, R&B/rap royalty, on his way to becoming a household name. *Nothing* debuted at number 21 on the US *Billboard* 200 chart, with first-week sales of 20,000 copies. Reviews were mainly harsh, some coming down hard on Pharrell's lyrics. "Pharrell Williams should either stop letting his wang co-write his songs or start giving it a credit in the liner notes," mocked *Rave* magazine, affording the album two and a half stars out of five.

Many reviews concluded that here was evidence of talents in artistic free-fall. "There isn't a lot on *Nothing* to indicate that these two guys were the same pair who once revolutionised the sound of hip hop," as Jayson Greene wrote for Pitchfork, although the review-aggregating website Metacritic deemed it worthy of an average score of 62, based on 19 reviews, which indicated a "generally favourable" judgment. The fact that, to date, N★E★R★D haven't released an album since *Nothing*, however, either suggests that Pharrell hasn't found a reason good enough to interrupt his solo career, or that those negative reviews really did sting. And yet reports as recently as

November 2014, of a tear-stricken Tyler, the Creator, watching a momentarily reformed N★E★R★D performing 'Rockstar' at Odd Future's annual festival, Camp Flog Gnaw Carnival in Los Angeles, where they headlined alongside the likes of Mac Miller, Rick Ross and Action Bronson, show there is a demand for their return. Video footage captured at the event show the OF frontman with his hands over his face, apparently overcome with emotion, sobbing with joy. Then again, as *XXL* magazine pointed out, he might just have been really, really high.

In 2011, Chad Hugo, in a rare venture away from his partnership with Pharrell, worked on Beyoncé's 'I Care', a number 16 US single, with successful rap/R&B producer Jeff Bhasker. That year Pharrell coaxed Gloria Estefan, another Latina, out of retirement in order to work his magic after meeting her through their trainer at the gym. An excited Estefan took to Twitter to tell fans about her latest collaboration, *Little Miss Havana*, her first English-language album since 2003's *Unwrapped* and her 26th overall.

"I can't tell u how much I've enjoyed working with @ NeRdArMy!," she wrote, referring to Williams. "It's truly been a magical experience and a wonderfully natural process."

Once the album was completed, she tweeted: "We have a baby!" She added, so that there were no (pun intended) misconceptions: "No sex."

That same year, Williams, again without Hugo, was one of 15 producers listed on the credits of *Trespassing*, the second album by Adam Lambert, the runner-up on the eighth season of *American Idol* who became a huge-selling star, not to mention the frontman, in place of the late Freddie Mercury, of a latterday incarnation of rock band Queen. The album was released in May 2012, when it debuted at America's number one – the first time an openly gay artist had done so – and included two Williams co-writes: the title track, and 'Kickin' In'.

Throughout 2012, Williams worked with rappers Lupe Fiasco (on a collaborative project called Child Rebel Soldier, also involving Kanye West, that sadly has yet to see the light of day) and Mac Miller on the *Pink Slime* EP, on the tracks 'Onaroll' and 'Glow'. He contributed four tracks to Game's *California Republic* mix-tape, one to Wiz Khalifa's US number one album, *O.N.I.F.C.*, and one to Kendrick Lamar's highly acclaimed *Good Kid*, 'm.A.A.d. City', also a US number one album in October.

There was also an attempt to bring some hip hop lustre to the career of former teen pop idol Miley Cyrus, for her fourth album, *Bangerz*, on the tracks '4x4' and '#GetItRight'. Cyrus' specific intention was to bring some "dirty south hip hop" edge to proceedings. Actually, '4x4', featuring rapper Nelly, was a curious, but strangely brilliant and oddly addictive, new hybrid: hip hop-country. A borderline novelty square-dance, it opened with Pharrell's trademark four-beat intro – a trick that he has used over the years to start songs including 'Frontin'', 'Milkshake', 'Drop It Like It's Hot', 'Blurred Lines' and 'Happy' – and was so instantly infectious it could only be the work of someone with an innate understanding of what makes great pop. And also someone with a keen grasp of how to establish an artist's outsider credentials from the off: the song, a Pharrell composition and production, had Cyrus declaring, "I'm a female rebel, can't you tell?" as she banged on the car dashboard, chipped a nail and leant out the window, yelling and driving so fast she was in danger of "piss[ing] on myself". The former Disney child star had officially bid farewell to her clean-cut past. The song was later sampled by British indie rock band Alt-J for their 2014 single 'Hunger Of The Pine', and although mystifyingly it was never released as a single, it did peak at number 41 on the US *Billboard* Pop Digital Songs chart.

"It's about having fun; kind of how a 4x4 truck symbolises rebelliousness," offered Nelly. "You know, mashing out, wanting to ride with the bad boys."

The other Williams offering on *Bangerz* was '#GetItRight', a typically stylish breeze of a Pharrell track that included whistling and a choppy guitar riff. Not dissimilar to the work of Michael Jackson and Prince circa 'Kiss', it was a song about sex that expressed Cyrus' desire to be categorised alongside older, more credible artists, although its very catchiness almost worked against it. As Heather Phares from AllMusic wrote in her review of the track, "[It's] so bouncy it almost sounds innocent despite Miley's insistence that she wants to be naughty."

Bangerz debuted at number one in the States, as did Usher's seventh studio album, *Looking 4 Myself*, including two Pharrell collaborations: 'Hot Thing' (which featured Pharrell and rising rap star A$AP Rocky) and the sixties-influenced, Stax-revisited stomp of 'Twisted'. "It's nostalgic," admitted Usher, who also claimed his intention was to "modernise" retro-soul, like CeeLo Green and Andre 3000 before him and Bruno Mars after him.

Less successful, commercially, was *The Origin Of Love*, the third album from Lebanese-British performer Mika, who had a global hit in 2007 with the single 'Grace Kelly'. It only reached number 24 in the UK and 47 in the US, despite the presence of two Pharrell tracks: 'Celebrate' (which itself reached number 21 in the States on its release as a single, with production assistance from Nick Littlemore of Australian electro-pop duo Empire Of The Sun), and the lush, smooth groove of 'Tah Dah', one of those lesser-known Williams compositions that deserved wider appreciation.

In 2012 Pharrell also produced those other purveyors of camp dance-pop Scissor Sisters, whose second album, from 2006, coincidentally was also titled *Tah Dah*. But this time Williams was drafted in to help on their fourth album, *Magic Hour*, on the

LP highlight 'Inevitable'. Although it didn't quite reach the giddy heights of their self-titled 2004 debut album, which went nine times platinum in the UK alone and was that country's best-selling record of the year, it did make its way to number four in Britain and 35 in the US, where it also reached number one in the Dance/ Electronic Albums chart.

There were a number of recording sessions undertaken by Pharrell in 2011 that never saw the light of day. There was an unreleased session with Miguel Jontel Pimentel, more widely known, simply as Miguel, the inventive young R&B artist from Los Angeles whose second album, *Kaleidoscope Dream*, was critically acclaimed in 2012. He worked with that other teen-pop Justin, Bieber, on sessions for the 2012 album, *Believe*, but they didn't make the final cut. There were aborted collaborations with Katy Perry for her *California Dreams* EP, with Rihanna for her seventh album, *Unapologetic*, and with Robin Thicke on a Michael Jackson-esque soufflé called 'Another Life', two years before he teamed up with Pharrell for the rather more successful 'Blurred Lines'.

Two tracks that did see the light of day were the ones he produced for Frank Ocean, the member of the Odd Future rap collective who, in 2011, was hailed as the future of R&B. Ocean cited Williams as one of his "creative heroes" and was delighted that he agreed to co-produce the Stevie Wonder-ful 'Sweet Life' (issued as a single) and closing nine-minute epic 'End/Golden Girl' (featuring Tyler, The Creator) from Ocean's top three US and UK debut album *Channel Orange*, which came out in 2012 and was widely regarded in critical circles as the album of the year.

He had already worked with Beyoncé's younger sister Solange (who in 2014 achieved global notoriety following a wild altercation in an elevator with her sister's husband, Jay-Z) on her 2008 album *Sol-Angel And The Hadley St. Dreams*, on 'I Decided Parts 1 & 2', which sampled the hand-claps from The Supremes' 1964 hit

'Where Did Our Love Go' and was based, melody-wise, on '(Love Is Like A) Heat Wave' by Martha & The Vandellas. In 2011, he was said to be working with her once more, on the follow-up, although that third album has yet to materialise. As of November that year, however, things were looking good, and the music was said to have a dance, new wave-inspired sound.

"So excited my album is shaping up so well!" tweeted Solange. "My sessions here with Pharrell have been amazing."

It wasn't just pop music that got Pharrell busy in 2011: he composed the intro theme for *Chelsea Lately*, the late-night American comedy talk show hosted by Chelsea Handler, and he composed and produced the music for the 84th Academy Awards, with a little help from his friend, composer Hans Zimmer, the orchestrator responsible for the *Dark Knight Rises* and *Lion King* scores, among many others.

The incidental music as Jennifer Lopez and Cameron Diaz, Tina Fey and Bradley Cooper, Tom Cruise and Tom Hanks and others came on to hand out gongs was courtesy of Williams and Zimmer. But if anyone was going to be receiving awards over the next three years, it was Pharrell.

CHAPTER 8

O Lucky Man!

"When we found that groove, I felt like Indiana Jones - like, 'Wow, I just discovered the Ark of the Covenant!'"

– Nile Rodgers

By 2013, Pharrell Williams had been in the music industry long enough for young fans turned artists who grew up idolising him to begin soliciting his assistance in the recording studio.

One such N★E★R★D-o-phile was Earl Sweatshirt of scandalous Los Angeles rap troupe Odd Future. He and Pharrell collaborated on his second solo album, *Doris* (a number two US R&B/Hip Hop chart entry that summer), on the track 'Burgundy' (titled after the colour of Earl's grandmother's carpet), which also featured sometime Odd Future associate Vince Staples. There were also sessions for an Earl-Pharrell track called 'Feet', which remains unreleased. Apparently, Pharrell spent much of his time with Earl darting between LA studios – he was also busy in the one next door, simultaneously putting the finishing touches to a track he had been slaving over with Robin Thicke, by the name of 'Blurred Lines'. Somehow, he and partner Chad Hugo managed to find the time to finish 'Burgundy' – one report stated that Pharrell knocked out the wonky, murky beat for 'Burgundy' in just 20 minutes.

"It was tight," the 19-year-old rapper (real name: Thebe Neruda Kgositsile) told MTV News of his association with Pharrell. "It was cool working with him, but I wasn't obsessed with it. And then we did that one [the unreleased track] the next day and it was amazing. He's too good. He did that shit in, like, 20 minutes."

Another of the producers on the Earl album, Taiwo Hassan, of the duo Christian Rich, revealed that Pharrell dealt with the simultaneous production of two classic tracks with his customary ease. "Pharrell was in the next room making 'Blurred Lines' with Robin Thicke [although] we didn't know it was 'Blurred Lines' back then," Hassan explained. "He came in and was like, 'This is the slowest beat I ever did, it's like 60 bpm [beats per minute]. He literally walked out for 20 minutes and came back in.

"Chad [Hugo] was there, too," he added, astonished at the pair's productivity and strike rate. "It was a Neptunes session and he just came in with the beat and we were like, 'Holy shit, that's it.' Pharrell is having a great year."

I met Earl that summer at his apartment in LA, near the Hollywood Walk of Fame, for a series of interviews that ran in *MOJO* magazine and *The Sunday Times Culture*, and we discussed Williams. "I love P," he told me. "He's tight, man."

He recalled how startled he was to see Pharrell multitask so effortlessly, and what it was like to hear 'Blurred Lines' for the first time. "I'm outside having a cigarette and it came on and they played it dumb loud. I was like, 'Damn, this sounds like Michael Jackson!' And then it came out and now it's a record-breaking song. That was a good weekend for music. Pharrell is fucking... he's ridiculous. The shit that he accomplishes. The

Daft Punk song ['Get Lucky'], this Robin Thicke shit – he's so fuckin' tight. And he's doing my shit which isn't incredibly commercial but, like Clipse, it isn't huge but the people it hits really like it. He's a machine – he's like the Apple of music. He's an angel. Pharrell is not a human being. He's a fuckin' freak, dude."

Earl's OF compadre, Tyler Okonma aka Tyler, The Creator, also hooked up with Pharrell in 2013 for a track on his third album, *Wolf* (number one in the US R&B/Hip Hop chart). The song in question was 'IFHY', which was optimistically released as a single since the acronym stood for 'I Fucking Hate You'. Produced by Tyler but featuring Pharrell on angelic, ethereal harmonies three minutes in, 'IFHY' was a scabrous but eerily pretty exploration of the artist's tortured emotions, with a stunning, disconcerting video directed by Wolf Haley (a pseudonym for the blazingly talented Okonma) in which Tyler played a lovestruck doll, acting out scenes in a dollhouse with a plastic girlfriend. Pharrell was as impressed by Tyler as the latter was by his mentor.

"This guy @fucktyler is talent ungoverned... feral...creates with his self-appointed licence... sick music, lyrics and directs his videos," tweeted the Neptunes producer following the collaboration.

When I interviewed Tyler for the *Guardian Guide* in 2011, it was inevitable that his hero Pharrell would crop up in our conversation. "It's my favourite album ever," he said of N★E★R★D's *In Search Of...*, which he bought on its release in 2002, when he was just 11 years old. "I wanted to get the word 'Brain' tattooed on my arm," he said of the N★E★R★D debut album track, "but it'd be weird now because I know Pharrell and Chad. It'd be weird to have that there."

Could Tyler, I wondered, still consider The Neptunes heroes now that he had met them?

"I don't know," he replied. "Those dudes are awesome. They'll always be awesome."

There were also some familiar affiliations in 2013. There was another trip into the studio with Jay-Z, for his twelfth album, *Magna Carta… Holy Grail*, a number one album in Canada, the States and the UK that summer. There were two Pharrell tie-ins this time: 'BBC' (a regular cameo-fest featuring Nas, Justin Timberlake, Beyoncé, Swizz Beatz and Timbaland), and the single 'Oceans' featuring Frank Ocean, a joint production by Williams and Timbaland. Nelly's seventh album, *M.O.* (top five US R&B/ Hip Hop), may not have reunited the rapper with many of the eight-million-strong audience that brought his 2000 debut album, *Country Grammar* (it is said to have sold 23,000 copies to date), but it was a feast for Pharrell Williams fans, including as it did five Pharrell productions: 'Get Like Me', a Top 40 US R&B/ Hip Hop single in July, bearing the talents of both Pharrell and Nicki Minaj; 'IDGAF' featuring Pharrell and T.I.; 'Maryland, Massachusetts'; 'Rick James' featuring T.I.; and 'Shake Whatever', a deluxe version bonus track featuring Pharrell. He worked with rapper Noreaga for the first time since 2002's 'God's Favorite', on the album *Student Of The Game*, specifically the rambunctious 'The Problem (Lawwwddd)'. And he joined forces once again with Clipse's Pusha T., on his album *My Name Is My Name* (US R&B/Hip Hop number two), and the songs 'S.N.I.T.C.H.' and 'Suicide' featuring the Philadelphia-based rapper Ab-Liva, the latter track issued as a single the following year.

More mellifluous was Pharrell's contribution to John Legend's *Love In The Future*: a ballad entitled 'Aim High', which appeared on the iTunes deluxe version of the soul singer-songwriter's fourth album. On a similar retro-R&B tip, but more playful, were his contributions to the little-known, but Grammy-nominated, Mayer Hawthorne's third album, *Where Does This Door Go*.

he Billionaire Boys Club/Ice Cream flagship store opening in New York, on November 28, 2007. BRIAN ACH/WIREIMAGE

With N.E.R.D. at the 2008 SXSW music festival at Stubbs BBQ in Austin, Texas, March 14, 2008.

Three's company: Pharrell, Chad Hugo and Shay Haley at MTV Studios in New York City, July 15, 2008.

rasher: performing in Times Square, New York, September 2010. BEN HIDER/WIREIMAGE

With Helen Lasichanh at the 84th Annual Academy Awards Governors Ball, the Hollywood & Highland Center in Hollywood, February 26, 2012. KEVORK DJANSEZIAN/GETTY IMAGES

o's that lady? Pharrell points out *Vogue* editor-in-chief Anna Wintour (second right) at the Lanvin Ready-To-Wear Fall/Winter 2 show as part of Paris Fashion Week, March 2, 2012. PASCAL LE SEGRETAIN/GETTY IMAGES

Speaking during the ASCAP Rhythm & Soul Music Awards at The Beverly Hilton Hotel in Los Angeles, June 29, 2012.
FREDERICK M. BROWN/GETTY IMAGES

Performing at the Pure Nightclub, Caesars Palace, Las Vegas, to celebrate Memorial Day weekend on May 26, 2013.
ETHAN MILLER/GETTY IMAGES FOR PURE NIGHTCLUB

With Robin Thicke at the 2013 BET Awards at Nokia Theatre L.A. Live on June 30, 2013 in Los Angeles.
JASON MERRITT/GETTY IMAGES FOR BET

it & Tie: Pharrell and Justin Timberlake attend an after-party lowing the *GQ* Men of the Year awards at The Royal Opera use, London, September 3, 2013.
VID M. BENETT/GETTY IMAGES

At a screening of *Despicable Me 2* at the Landmark Theater in Los Angeles, November 19, 2013.
DAVID BUCHAN/GETTY IMAGES FOR THEWRAP

arrell and Helen Lasichanh in West Hollywood, California, November 21, 2013. JB LACROIX/WIREIMAGE

Got lucky: Thomas Bangalter (left) of Daft Punk and Pharrell attend the 56th Grammy Awards at Staples Center in Los Angeles, January 26, 2014. MICHAEL KOVAC/WIREIMAGE

Party people: Pharrell and Paul McCartney at the 56th Grammy Awards. KEVIN MAZUR/WIREIMAGE

Showing you how to hustle: at the BRIT Awards, 02 Arena, London, February 19, 2014. DAVID M. BENETT/GETTY IMAGES

the BET Awards, June 29, 2014. MICHAEL TRAN/FILMMAGIC

Meet the Williams: Helen, Pharrell and son Rocket Ayer attend the ceremony honouring Pharrell with a star on the Hollywood Walk of Fame in Hollywood, California, December 4, 2014. CHELSEA LAUREN/WIREIMAGE

mer coach on *The Voice*, CeeLo Green, poses with current coaches Christina Aguilera, Blake Shelton, Adam Levine and Pharrell at Pacific Design Center in West Hollywood, California, April 23, 2015. TRAE PATTON/NBC VIA GETTY IMAGES

He got the cream: at the 57th Annual Grammy Awards in Los Angeles, February 8, 2015. JEFF VESPA/WIREIMAGE

Tracks such as 'Reach Out Richard', 'Wine Glass Woman', 'The Stars Are Ours' and 'They Don't Know You' were Steely Danish melodic delights deserving of a wider audience – the album faltered commercially, just scraping the Top 30 in the US, and reaching a disappointing number 58 in the UK.

Pharrell also produced a remix by an exciting new kind of soul artist, Canada's Abel Tesfaye, who operates as The Weeknd – his version of 'Wanderlust', from the *Kiss Land* album, evinced his determination to keep abreast of contemporary developments, although it also nodded to the past, with some of the disco sheen of Patrice Rushen's 1982 post-disco classic, 'Forget Me Nots'. And to prove that he would work outside his US/North American comfort zone, he briefly entered the studio with British rapper/grime artist Tinie Tempah, although the results remain unreleased.

Ever darting from project to project and style to style, Pharrell, in tandem with Heitor Pereira, composed the original music to *Despicable Me 2*, which was promoted with the songs 'Just A Cloud Away', 'Scream' (featuring CeeLo Green) and the rather more successful 'Happy'. And Williams and Hans Zimmer wrote the score for the new Superman movie, *Man Of Steel*. Classic FM previewed the recording, remarking on the "drum battle" taking place in the studio for the occasion, guided by Zimmer in a SuperHans T-shirt, with such legendary sticksmen (and women) as Josh Freese (who has worked with Nine Inch Nails, The Vandals and Devo), Sheila E (who famously played on many of Prince's albums), Jason Bonham, son of Led Zeppelin drummer John, and Pharrell himself, all of whom appeared in a special video detailing the process of recording percussion for *Man Of Steel*. The soundtrack did well in the charts, entering at number nine and selling 32,000 copies in its first week. The critics were less kind, however, many dismissing it as repetitive, simplistic and over-reliant on those drums. There was the odd positive review, notably from Allmusic, which called the soundtrack "grittier and darker than any of its predecessors, due in large part to Zimmer's proclivity for non-stop, thunderous percussion", and from Jørn Tillnes of Soundtrackgeek, who raved: "The purists, the soundtrack geeks of old, will no doubt hate this score and will use every ounce of their energy to bash it as nothing more than generic droning music. For the rest of us, I believe the new bold direction the Superman franchise is taking is both brilliant and brave. Superman deserves this score and so do you."

But by far the most highly praised of Pharrell's 2013 adventures in stereo was his collaboration with Daft Punk for their long-awaited fourth studio album, *Random Access Memories*, a US number one that May. He co-wrote two tracks for the album with Daft Punk's Thomas Bangalter and Guy-Manuel de Homem-Christo: 'Lose Yourself To Dance' and 'Get Lucky', the latter also involving the writing skills of Nile Rodgers, the legendary guitarist and co-songwriter (with bassist Bernard Edwards) in the premier group of the disco era, Chic.

Williams first heard about Daft Punk's latest studio foray, one that had begun in earnest at least 18 months earlier, "at a Madonna party". There, he immediately offered his services.

"If you just want me to play tambourine, I'll do it," he joked, referring to the pair as "the robots" because of their tendency to appear in public in robot helmets to preserve their anonymity and mystique. Daft Punk and Williams later met in Paris, where he shared some of his own material.

As Thomas Bangalter explained to *Vibe* magazine, in a joint interview with Pharrell, Daft Punk were long-term fans of his work and output as a producer, rapper and musician.

"But what we really appreciate more than anything," he said, "is a multitalented artist that has a strong aura and is super-talented, charismatic and very glamorous. His natural glamour – he is as elegant in jeans [as he is] in a tuxedo."

Bangalter referred to Pharrell's ubiquity, but stressed that this didn't mean he would be redundant in years to come, a flavour of the month likely to lose its taste. "He would totally be [relevant] 30, 40 years ago as well," insisted the French producer. "He has that timeless quality of what a great entertainer is."

As for Williams, asked when he first heard the French duo's music, he recalled that it was midway through a conversation with a woman he'd just met. "All of a sudden I heard a song and was like, 'What the fuck is that?'" he reminisced, describing the sound he heard as "like something regal, something very royal and different, from a higher caliber. When that guy sang 'One More Time', I was like, 'What the?!' And then it was everywhere. Like, I heard it in cars in the hood. From that point I was in love with the sound and the groove. Isn't that the most amazing feeling when we hear something and ask, 'What is it?'"

The interviewer from *Vibe* wanted to discuss some of the many artists with whom Pharrell had been collaborating of late – Kendrick Lamar, Frank Ocean, Robin Thicke, Miley Cyrus – but he declined, saying, "I want to spend this time talking about 'the robots'. It's a rare opportunity, because they don't [usually] talk to people."

He was more than happy to discuss Nile Rodgers, however. "I'm kind of in a Nile Rodgers place right now," he said in an episode of *The Collaborators*. This was a series of promotional videos designed to accompany the release of *Random Access Memories* – other artists filmed for the occasion included electronic dance music pioneer Giorgio Moroder and the cult songwriter Paul Williams, just two of the many guest artists on the album (the others were Julian Casablancas of indie rock band The Strokes, US house and garage producer Todd Edwards, eclectic Canadian musician Chilly Gonzales, and Noah Lennox aka Panda Bear of experimental outfit Animal Collective).

Daft Punk were taken aback by Pharrell's seemingly throwaway comment about Rodgers, because they had already begun talks to solicit the involvement in *RAM* of the Chic legend, whose landmark productions, with his late partner Edwards, had proven so influential on Williams growing up. "On two sides of the Atlantic, we were in the same place," marvelled Pharrell of his and Daft Punk's synchronous ideas. "It was, 'Let's go back to that magical time when music and the liveliness of music are what moved people.'"

Pharrell explained that, feeling fatigued during their meeting in Paris, the Daft Punk droids offered him a pill, "more on the holistic side of things", and as soon as he took it he felt "a burst of energy". That was when work began on the two *RAM* tracks – Williams recalled that the duo were keen to get everything just right in the studio, especially during the recording of the vocals for 'Get Lucky', when he was asked to perform several takes and numerous attempts were made to finesse certain phrases.

They told him to "sing it again, again, again", Pharrell recounted in *Rolling Stone*. "Then I did four or five more takes, they picked what they liked, then I sang each of those parts over and over. The robots are perfectionists."

The website Stereogum tried to push Pharrell on the details of the sessions that produced 'Get Lucky'. Was it, they enquired, a collaborative process? "When they brought me in the studio, that track was done," he replied. "They just asked me to write on it." He added, somewhat vaguely, that, "after an hour so", the track had been written, give or take a few retakes, to get it absolutely right.

"The song," added Pharrell, "kind of wrote itself."

The end result became the centrepiece of Daft Punk's magnum opus, *Random Access Memories*. However, by the time Pharrell was on the plane back to America, he had, he said, "forgotten everything". And "still to this day," he continued, with a sly, teasing grin, "I couldn't figure out, was it the jet lag or did they hit me with the Men In Black [i.e. the ray that cancels out all memories, from the 1997 comedy sci-fi movie]?"

The next time Williams heard 'Get Lucky', he did so "with fresh ears". He was blown away by this masterpiece of melody and sublime musicianship, one that harked back to a pre-digital age when musicians pored over every detail of their performances and attention was paid to capturing the perfect rendition.

"Perfect" is the operative word: Daft Punk hired choirs, string sections, trumpeters and pedal-steel players, they drafted in session pros who had worked on Michael Jackson's *Thriller* and *Off The Wall*, they flew between recording studios in New York and Los Angeles, "to capture the unique sounds and vibes of the classic rooms" as *Rolling Stone* put it. Wherever they went, they kept the mics running, to capture the freewheeling jams that they edited later using Pro Tools, conjuring songs out of the footage "like we were making a film," Bangalter said, explaining that certain songs on the album spanned two and a half years and five different studios.

Pharrell could scarcely believe the songs or his own involvement in *RAM*, especially 'Get Lucky' and the way he sang over that rhythm, one that seemed to be simultaneously beamed in from the future and exquisitely redolent of the past. What particularly impressed him was that it took two "robots" to create a pulse that reminded him of the human heartbeat.

"It reminded me of some kind of exotic island," he said of the finished article and the feelings it aroused. "Not sure if it was this planet or not, but it just felt like a place where it was forever four in the morning, and because you're on an island you could see the sun rising in the sky – you know, that peachy colour."

The music, he added, elaborating on the sensation of being exposed to this magical music for the first time, was "as alive as the air was".

"Getting lucky," he further elucidated, was not just about meeting a woman and then sleeping with her. No, it was about meeting someone for the first time and "clicking". "There's no better fortune in this existence, to me," he said.

Asked by the interviewer in online series The Collaborators who he imagined listening to 'Get Lucky' with, he replied instantly, "Oh, my girl," presumably referring to his longtime partner, model/designer Helen Lasichanh, whom he would marry later that year, on October 12, 2013. "We would be in a car, pulled up to the side of the beach, and just let[ting] it play. This music is beyond. You don't need [the drug] MDMA for this music, cos the music is so incredibly vivid."

People, he considered, had "lost respect for the groove" in recent years, and music had become overly clinical and synthetic. He decided that it was missing what he called "the gut". Overcome with excitement at this glorious new music, he talked in enraptured, rarefied terms.

"Somewhere outside of the ether that we exist in there is a multitude of realms of possibility and alternate directions and I think they [Daft Punk] just went in those libraries and dusted off those things," he said with a dreamy sigh.

He described the sound they achieved as "like the mid-seventies/early eighties of a different universe and dimension, not of this one. This music represents the freedom of all human beings. This is for the globe."

People from six to 66-year-olds could enjoy Daft Punk's expansive, inclusive new sound. Where, wondered the interviewer, could Daft Punk possibly proceed from here?

"Up," replied Pharrell, "where they belong. We're lucky to have them on this planet. They could just get back on the spaceship that brought them here, and go, leave us. But they're gracious; they're nice robots. They chose to stay."

It was one of the great musical unions of recent times: Nile Rodgers, Daft Punk and Pharrell Williams, three supreme exponents of shimmery dance music; several generations of genius. They were destined to work together: Daft Punk first met Rodgers at a listening party in New York for the duo's 1997 debut album, *Homework*, and thereafter became friends. The duo acknowledged Chic's influence on their music, but a series of scheduling conflicts put the kibosh on any plans to collaborate. Eventually, they invited Rodgers to the *Random Access Memories* sessions at Electric Lady Studios in New York City – the very studios where the first Chic single, 'Everybody Dance', had been recorded in 1977, in the very area where Rodgers grew up. But it wasn't until Pharrell added his lead vocal melody, and doused the project in evanescent soulfulness, that true perfection was achieved.

In the video to 'Get Lucky', as they performed the song against the kind of peachy sunset Pharrell had dreamed about, the four resembled a sort of ultimate 21st century pop group. In an interview with Rodgers that I did for *The Guardian* in 2013, for an article entitled Disco Gets Lucky, he was ecstatic to be involved in the record, and laughed that Daft Punk were thinking along similar lines during filming.

"It's funny you say that, because while we were doing the video they [Daft Punk] kept saying, 'This is like our dream band – we got our guitar player and our lead singer!'"

Was Pharrell – a singer, songwriter, producer-auteur and mogul – the latterday incarnation of Rodgers, the self-styled CEO of the Chic Organization? "I can't make superlative statements when it comes to music, I don't believe in that, they're just opinions and my opinion is not a fact," he replied. "I can't say that. But I certainly know he's done a damn fine job."

Rodgers recalled meeting Williams at the Grammy awards ceremony in 2003, just after the latter had received acclaim for his production of Justin Timberlake's 'Rock Your Body', whose similarity to Chic's 'Good Times' was a matter of record. "He knew that I knew, obviously, and he bowed down and said, 'Hey, man, thank you,'" he recalled with pride.

In the *Guardian* interview Rodgers, only recently given the all-clear on the aggressive prostate cancer with which he had been diagnosed in 2011, admitted to his delight at having been invited into the studio with the French producers. "We caught each other at the exact right moment," he said. "I happened to be in New York, they called me up, they came to my apartment, and they spoke holistically and conceptually about the record, and that was it. It was great – totally like love at first sight."

Rodgers alluded to the sessions that created David Bowie's hugely popular *Let's Dance* album in 1983, of which he was producer. "Daft Punk were just like Bowie: he let me do what I do, and these guys let me do what I do. They loved it. They said, 'Go ahead, Nile, do your thing, man.'"

He was as happy for Daft Punk as he was for himself at the unprecedented global success of 'Get Lucky'. "It couldn't have happened to nicer guys. I want to see them succeed more than I want to succeed. Up till now, Daft Punk maybe had a number one with 'One More Time' [2000 single], but that's only one. I've had a lot around the world," said the producer of massive hits for Chic as well as for Madonna, Bowie and Duran Duran. "So it's really important to me but honestly I feel much more happy about it for them. And that's me being 100 percent honest."

He furthered that Daft Punk's success was even more deserved because it was based on a risk – at the height of the prominence of EDM (electronic dance music), *Random Access Memories* was a triumph of good old-fashioned sample-free musicianship. He described 'Get Lucky' as Chic 2.0, not least because it was recorded at the old Chic studios, "literally three blocks from where I grew up – that's my old neighbourhood," he said. 'Get Lucky' was disco revisited, quintessential disco, a latterday disco pinnacle. I asked him what exactly it was, sonically and in terms of atmosphere, that made disco disco, and he replied: "For me, what makes disco 'disco' is the feeling. You can play R&B and jazz and it not be disco, and you can play disco and it be jazzy and R&B and funky. It incorporates all those elements.

"It's almost like pornography," he decided. "There was a famous trial in America where they were trying to define pornography, and I believe that the judge said, 'I can't define pornography but I know it when I see it.' Well, I can't define disco, but I know it when I hear it!"

Pharrell wasn't convinced that 'Get Lucky' was disco, preferring the term "post-disco", because, being literal, the track wasn't made in the late-seventies, it was made in 2012-13, and disco, of all pop music genres, was wholly mired in a specific time period.

Thomas Bangalter went for a vaguer definition of the song. "It's something as simple as music that makes us feel good and makes people feel good," he said. Comparing Chic's brand of disco to their own, he continued: "Nile made music in the seventies and the eighties that made people feel good. And it's us and Pharrell that make people feel good in the nineties and noughties. That's four different decades. It feels like the four of us are teaming up and playing music for the fifth decade. At some point we can still recognise Nile's guitar, Pharrell's voice; but somehow it's a little bit of a different twist on it. And it has both that familiarity that feels like you've heard it before, and then there's something new, like music you could hear [today] that encapsulates those things. Trying to focus on happiness in a very essential way can become some kind of a bigger statement."

With 'Get Lucky', Daft Punk and Pharrell were paying homage to a music that was hard to define, but was obviously disco. "It wasn't a love letter or even an homage to Chic specifically," countered Rodgers in his *Guardian* interview with me from 2013, "but rather it was a recognition of those records and how they made you feel."

He noted that playing with actual living musicians, as opposed to using machines, was a novel experience for Daft Punk. "If you listen to Guy-Manuel and Thomas talk, it's as though it's the first time they've ever done this," he said. "Whereas every record I've ever made has been the result of going into recording studios to interact with other musicians.

"There is something unbelievably pleasant about this type of music that you can't define," added Rodgers. "All you can do is react and get caught up in the emotion of it, and in the absolute bliss of the grooves, at the risk of sounding corny."

He described 'Get Lucky' as "a futuristic record that looks back" and revealed that, in the last month, he had listened to it every day "and found new nuggets of gold in it every time".

"I listened," he said, "to the brilliance of what I call its 'complex simplicity'. 'Get Lucky' makes you feel so incredible, and it has pulled off that complex simplicity in wonderfully rewarding ways."

There was a time when disco was derided – at its height in the late-seventies, detractors even launched a campaign against it called "Disco Sucks", with record-burning assemblies and angry mobs wielding placards. The success of 'Get Lucky' was, in a way, the revenge of disco.

"I'm not a negative person, so I'd hate to look at it like that," Rodgers offered, tentatively, "but it is hard not to feel some pleasure at its success, because certainly my band [Chic] were held up as arch-enemies at one point – the arch-enemies of rock'n'roll! When 'Good Times' [Chic's 1979 single] got to number one, it was good because it felt like the entire industry was against us."

Now, by contrast, disco had been rediscovered, rehabilitated and afforded new respect.

"It's like *Raiders Of The Lost Ark*, like uncovering something from the past that has tremendous significance," he mused. "It took Daft Punk, Pharrell and I getting together to reveal the truth! When we found that groove, I felt like Indiana Jones - like, 'Wow, I just discovered the Ark of the Covenant!'"

Rodgers was awed by Daft Punk's musical achievement. He marvelled, too, at the way they unveiled their new sonic vision, which Rodgers termed, paradoxically, "old school". Before its release, 'Get Lucky' was revealed via two 15-second television advertisements broadcast during US TV's comedy show *Saturday Night Live*, after which Rodgers and Williams announced their involvement in the track. Various fan remixes of the clips thereafter appeared online. A third trailer was shown at the Coachella Valley Music and Arts Festival, featuring Daft Punk, Pharrell and Rodgers.

"That part of it I do find interesting," Rodgers told me. "The big thing about Daft Punk's overriding concept was to treat the global marketing strategy as if the internet didn't exist. It was all shot on beautiful big format film. And the marketing was boots-on-the-ground, all billboards, print, radio and television – old school. There was a real sense of event."

After it leaked in mid-April, 'Get Lucky' was released as a digital download on April 19. Before long, it had reached number one in more than 40 countries. To date, it has sold upwards of 10 million copies, putting it in the singles superleague, where it joins the likes of Adele's 'Someone Like You', Lady Gaga's 'Born This Way' and Eminem's 'Lose Yourself'. In the UK, it entered the singles chart at number three, becoming Daft Punk's first Top 10 hit there since 'One More Time', then reached the top, the duo's first ever number one single in Britain. By late May 2013, over 600,000 copies had been sold, making it the nation's best-selling single of the year up to that point. By June, that figure had reached one million, making it the first song involving either Daft Punk, Williams or Rodgers to achieve this feat. It was eventually the second best-selling song in the UK in 2013 with sales of 1,308,007 copies, runner-up to Robin Thicke's 'Blurred Lines', another Pharrell collaboration.

In the US, the song debuted at number five on the *Billboard* Dance/Electronic Songs chart and by the start of June had reached number one, remaining on top for 13 weeks. It peaked at number two on the mainstream chart for five weeks, behind 'Blurred Lines', making Pharrell the first artist to simultaneously occupy the top two slots of the *Billboard* Hot 100 chart since 2009, when The Black Eyed Peas achieved the same feat.

The song also broke records with the highest number of plays of any song in a single day on music streaming site Spotify; it became the most streamed track of 2013 in the UK. Meanwhile, 'Get Lucky' was nominated for Best Song of the Summer at the 2013 MTV Video Music Awards and it received awards for both Best Pop Duo/Group Performance and Record of the Year at the 56th Annual Grammy Awards. It won Track of the Year in a Digital Spy readers' poll and in the *Village Voice*'s prestigious Pazz & Jop annual critics' poll.

There were numerous remixes and cover versions that ran the gamut of styles and languages. English folk and indie bands Daughter, Peace and Mystery Jets recorded versions, as did Dutch reggae/hip hop band the Postmen, US rappers The Roots, American country-rock band Wilco and UK grime producer Naughty Boy. Israeli musician Noy Alooshe made a mashup of the song with Michael Jackson's 'Billie Jean'. On BBC TV's talent show *The Voice*, judges Tom Jones, Jessie J, will.i.am and Danny O'Donoghue of The Script sang the song. There were even iterations from British comedians Simon Pegg and Nick Frost and by the Russian Interior Ministry Choir for the opening ceremony of the 2014 Winter Olympics in Sochi.

But perhaps the most memorable take on 'Get Lucky' came courtesy of Stephen Colbert, host of US satirical TV show *The Colbert Report*. Daft Punk were scheduled to appear on the August 6 episode to promote *Random Access Memories*, but were unable to do so due to contractual obligations regarding their future appearance at the 2013 MTV Video Music Awards. According to Colbert, the duo were unaware of any exclusivity agreement and were prevented from appearing by MTV executives the morning prior to the taping of the programme. Colbert snapped into action, using their non-appearance as an opportunity to corral a number of actors, musicians, presenters and politicians – including Hugh Laurie, Jeff Bridges, Jimmy Fallon, The Rockettes, Bryan Cranston, Jon Stewart, Matt Damon and Henry Kissinger – for an alternative, and hilarious, performance of what Colbert had declared on his show to be "the Song of the Summer of the Century".

The critics were unanimous in their praise. Michael Cragg from *The Guardian* hailed it "the best thing Pharrell Williams has been involved with for a long time". Pitchfork included it as a Best New Track, stating that the song's "real elegance lies in the hands of Nile Rodgers". Lewis Corner from Digital Spy awarded it five stars and said that Daft Punk's "creative methods may be unorthodox, [yet] the final result is a legal rush we can all enjoy". Sasha Frere-Jones of *The New Yorker* wrote that Rodgers' performance in the song was "as close to magic as pop comes". *Rolling Stone* reviewer Will Hermes gave it four out of five and described it as "an old-school disco jam", calling it "formidable". To Amy Sciarretto of PopCrush it was an "intoxicating track" and "all that's right with electronic music". Radio hosts and DJs got in on the act. BBC Radio 1's Annie Mac deemed it "real music to dance to". And British DJ and producer Norman Cook (alias Fatboy Slim) told *The Daily Star*: "I'm so impressed by [Daft Punk]. It's a breath of fresh old school air. They have given us [electronic musicians] all a kick up the arse."

It was British journalist Caitlin Moran who best captured the heady thrill, and the sheer joyous ubiquity, of 'Get Lucky', in an article for *The Times* entitled "My addiction to the Daft Punk song of the summer". In it, she reflected on the song's appeal, suggesting it was due to its combination of minor chords and regular disco-type "up" danceability – what Nile Rodgers in his *Guardian* interview with me termed "that ineffable sense of melancholy", which was in stark contrast to Pharrell's lyrics about "good fun" and being "up all night".

"I am absolutely capable of both working and listening to 'Get Lucky' without any impairment of my faculties," Moran wrote. "This is because, for the past three weeks, I've been doing everything while listening to 'Get Lucky': working, parenting, cooking, being drunk. I am informed by iTunes that I've listened to it 113 times. It's taken over my life. I'd call for help, but it's the happiest I've been since Amy Winehouse's *Back To Black* came out in 2006."

Rodgers was as overwhelmed as anyone by its sheer domination of people's lives that summer. "When I think how it happened, too, with people who I like a lot, that we just decided to go into the studio and do something," he said. "And then it turns out like this? It's absolutely remarkable, because no one was prepared for this!

"I've had big records and number ones; I have had records that were number one in the United States but nowhere else... I've had records which have done well [in the UK], but not in the States," he continued. "But to have this ubiquitous record, that is a hit everywhere... It's amazing to me. I'm out on the road and I can hear it wherever I go. I'm flabbergasted!"

The dream team of Rodgers, Pharrell and Daft Punk joined forces again for another track on *Random Access Memories*, 'Lose Yourself To Dance'. It was the sixth track on the album, but the second paean to music itself, the other being album opener 'Give Life Back To Music'. It was also the second single, lifted from the album in August 2013. It was slower than its predecessor, and didn't match its phenomenal success, charting lower and in fewer countries; nevertheless, it continued the reign of *RAM* throughout the summer of 2013.

Daft Punk revealed that the song was the result of a desire to create dance music with live drummers. Thomas Bangalter elaborated that they wished to redefine dance music as "something lighter or something more [primal]", and that the song was designed to evoke communal dance-floor rapture. Pharrell was more specific, stating that the song made him feel "like walking down the street in the middle of the night in London and it's 1984, 1985. I don't hear the seventies in that at all." He added that David Bowie could theoretically have sung the song, possibly alluding to the lustrous funk sound achieved by producer Nile Rodgers on Bowie's *Let's Dance* album.

'Lose Yourself To Dance' was typical of the music on *Random Access Memories* in that numerous top-class session musicians were employed to perform on it (notwithstanding the sound effect of machines singing created by Daft Punk's use of vocoders). Instrumentalists included Nile Rodgers on rhythm guitar, Nathan East on bass guitar, and John "J.R." Robinson on drums. East was a founder member of contemporary jazz quartet Fourplay and had recorded, performed and co-written songs with the likes of Eric Clapton, Michael Jackson, Joe Satriani, George Harrison, Phil Collins, Stevie Wonder, Toto and Herbie Hancock. And Robinson was no slouch when it came to stellar associations, having worked with Quincy Jones on Michael Jackson's *Off The*

Wall album and the charity single 'We Are The World', as well as with Chaka Khan, Lionel Richie, Mike Oldfield and Madonna. It may not have sold in the same vast quantities as 'Get Lucky', but 'Lose Yourself To Dance' was a similarly magical piece of music, and part of what was universally regarded as the album of the year: the record that revolutionised 21st century dance music by reaffirming 20th century values. This was history, as it happened.

"Think about it," said Williams, swept away by it all. "Right now, you're in the middle of what was and what is about to be. Do you know how important now is? All of this is unbelievable. I'm pinching myself."

Vibe magazine's Sarah Polonsky wondered how Daft Punk managed to assemble such an exceptional cast of musicians for *Random Access Memories*, and how they summoned the nerve to ditch all the high-tech gadgetry at their disposal. Pharrell replied, in a roundabout way. "You have to love music," he said. "You have to love the musicians that pontificated [sic] and decided to put it on tape. When you listened to this album, you were listening to two huge fans working with people they have admired all their lives. And that is one of the biggest things that I have an incredible admiration for when it comes to them because they have the willingness to stare all of the contemporary and modern equipment in the face and go, 'I will not use your preset. You will not lock me in this box.'"

Giorgio Moroder, one of the musicians and collaborators on *Random Access Memories* (on the track 'Giorgio By Moroder'), and the man who almost single-handedly invented modern electronic dance music in 1977 as producer and co-writer of the Donna Summer single 'I Feel Love', talked in his episode of The Collaborators about "the human touch" that Daft Punk and the many musicians on *RAM* brought to bear on the project. Thomas Bangalter referred to it as "that energy", one that was essential for what they set out to achieve.

"We wanted to do dance music with live musicians," he affirmed. "The process – the arrangement, calling, production on these instrumental tracks – was new for us, but there was so much life and energy from the music performances themselves."

His partner, de Homem-Christo, explained that on 'Get Lucky', for example, Nile Rodgers would play his guitar part, and then guitarist Paul Jackson Jr. (a veteran from Michael Jackson's *Thriller*, *Bad* and *Dangerous* albums) would "feed off" the energy from Rodgers' playing, after which the keyboardist and bassist would chime in, jamming with the Chic legend, all adding to the atmosphere of unbridled creativity and meticulous musicianship. "By the time we connected with Pharrell to finish writing the song," he said, "it was infused with so much performance that it became the easiest song to write to. It became this timeless piece."

With 'Lose Yourself To Dance', Daft Punk were, according to Homem-Christo, attempting to create "this idea of a timeless place or dance floor where you can lose yourself. The idea of unity of the dance floor, people being connected."

Bangalter termed it "handmade dance music". And yet he considered 'Lose Yourself To Dance' different to 'Get Lucky' in that it was "more essential and original". "It's really about what dancing is – people interacting and what the dance floor is," he said. It made him think of another dance record; a dance record by Pharrell. "In the same way that 'Drop It Like It's Hot', where you hear the sounds and are like, 'Wow!' It's interesting to experiment with what the dance floor can be. Like, how can you be turned on to the act of dancing at a time where dance music is done with a drum machine and computers? There's not a point to challenge that. One of the important things for us in this record is that it's done with live musicians and it comes out at the time in dance and pop music where no one [else] does that."

Ultimately, Daft Punk – and Pharrell – were doing what they wanted to do, and doing it in their own unique way. It just so happened that what they were doing coincided with the tastes of most of the western world. No wonder they were being afforded the highest accolades imaginable. Not that they would ever be swayed from their path of true self-expression.

"The only pressure is our pressure," said Bangalter. "To me, and I think it's the same for Pharrell, we're just friends and we're all professionals. So people that like what we do or what Pharrell does call us genius, but we really don't care for the term. We just like what we do."

'Get Lucky' and 'Lose Yourself To Dance', Pharrell's contributions to *Random Access Memories*, helped propel the album to the top of charts around the world, from Australia to Estonia, Poland to Japan, and sell eight million copies. At the 56th Annual Grammy Awards, it won in the Album of the Year, Best Dance/Electronica Album and Best Engineered Album, Non-Classical categories. Reviewers were breathless in their praise: "By some margin Daft Punk's best album in a career that's already redefined dance music at least twice. It is, in short, a mind blower" (Q magazine); "*Random Access Memories* breathes life into the safe music that dominates today's charts, with its sheer ambition" (*The Independent*); "A headphones album in an age of radio singles; a bravura live performance that stands out against pro forma knob-twiddling; a jazzy disco attack on the basic house beat; a full collaboration at a time when the superstar DJ stands alone. If EDM is turning humans into robots, Daft Punk are working hard to make robot pop feel human again" (*Entertainment Weekly*).

As usual, Pharrell took it all in his stride. For him, the success, both critical and commercial, wasn't due to him so much as it was thanks to an openness on the part of the public – and the Almighty.

"First and foremost I look at it like… the people," he contended. "They vote for the songs, they share the songs with their friends, they stream the songs, they talk about the songs, and they purchase the songs. And without that type of reaction there is no 'huge', there is no 'big', there is no 'successful'. If you're successful it just means that the people spoke. So I'm sort of indebted to the people. And personally, I'm indebted to God and the universe for giving me the time. Without time, opportunity means nothing. All those things are factors for me."

Still, even he admitted that *Random Access Memories* – and 'Get Lucky' in particular – had been amazing achievements. These weren't so much record releases as cultural phenomena. But what was arguably most amazing about 'Get Lucky' was that it wasn't even Pharrell Williams' most successful single of that year.

CHAPTER 9

The Thicke Of It

"We tried to do everything that was taboo"

— Robin Thicke.

If the appeal of 'Get Lucky' was immediate, then 'Blurred Lines' was more insidious. The lead single from the album of the same name by an American-Canadian singer-songwriter called Robin Thicke, featuring Pharrell Williams and rapper Clifford Joseph Harris, Jr. aka T.I., it was actually released — by The Neptunes' imprint Star Trak — three weeks before the Daft Punk single, but it seemed to take a little longer to take hold. In the US, the song's progress was slow but sure. It debuted at number 94 on the *Billboard* Hot 100; the following week it rose to number 89, then to number 70, then to number 54. It appeared to want to stick around the middle of the charts until, in mid-May, Thicke and Pharrell performed the song live on NBC's *The Voice*. That had the effect of catapulting it up to number 12.

Eventually, 'Blurred Lines' would overtake 'Get Lucky' to become one of the best-selling singles of all time, with sales of 14.8 million — in the States, it topped the *Billboard* Hot 100 for

12 consecutive weeks, making it the longest-running number one not just of 2013 but of the 2010s, surpassing Rihanna's 'We Found Love' (2011). It wasn't superseded until Mark Ronson's 'Uptown Funk' in 2015.

At one point – June 29, 2013, to be precise – Pharrell Williams, who was involved in the song's writing and production, became only the twelfth artist in US music history to simultaneously hold the top two positions in the chart, with 'Blurred Lines' and 'Get Lucky', respectively. Peaking at number one meant it was Williams' third *Billboard* Hot 100 chart-topper after 'Drop It Like It's Hot' with Snoop Dogg in 2004 and 'Money Maker' with Ludacris in 2006; it reached number one in over two dozen further countries, including the UK and Germany, two of the most commercially significant territories outside of the US.

It launched Thicke on the international stage, too, becoming easily his most successful song: it was his first chart entry since 2009's 'Sex Therapy' and only his second Top 20 entry ever, after 2007's 'Lost Without U' peaked at number 14. It also worked well for T.I., becoming his fourth Hot 100 number one after 'My Love' with Justin Timberlake in 2006, and his own singles 'Whatever You Like' and 'Live Your Life' in 2008.

It was the best-selling digital single of 2013 worldwide, and remains the second best-selling digital single of all time, behind The Black Eyed Peas' 2009 hit 'I Gotta Feeling'. And it broke the record for the largest radio audience in history – by July 2013, it had reached more than 242.65 million listeners, even reputedly racking up spins on some country stations. It was nominated for two Grammy Awards, for Record of the Year and Best Pop Duo/ Group Performance.

It was as stratospherically successfully as it was universally controversial – but that came later. For the first few months of its dominance of the airwaves, it was merely the latest, and seemingly greatest if its sales were any measure, demonstration of Pharrell Williams' unerring ability to give the public what they wanted in terms of music, lyrics, melody, and groove.

Thicke and Williams had worked together before – on the former's second album, 2006's *The Evolution Of Robin Thicke*, Pharrell had been executive producer and The Neptunes were producers of the lead single, 'Wanna Love You Girl', although it failed to chart. Not wishing to luck out this time, the pair entered the studio with the intention of recreating the exuberant party atmosphere of Marvin Gaye's 'Got To Give It Up', a US number one from 1977 and Thicke's favourite song. It apparently took them anything between 30 minutes and an hour to come up with the track.

"Pharrell and I were in the studio and I told him that one of my favourite songs of all time was Marvin Gaye's 'Got To Give It Up'," Thicke told *GQ*. "I was like, 'Damn, we should make something like that, something with that groove.'"

They started with Pharrell randomly singing, "Hey, hey, hey!" – soon, they had their song.

"We literally wrote it in about a half hour and recorded it. The whole thing was done in a couple [of] hours – normally, those are the best ones," said Thicke, who remembers having a great time in the studio, "dancing around like old men. We were doing our old men barbecue dances."

They had no idea what a monster they had created. "We felt like maybe it was something special but it was so different. We didn't know it would be this big," said Thicke, who modestly put a lot of the song's success down to his writing partner and producer. "Pharrell, being one of the great hitmakers of the last 20 years, he really has an amazing ability, like a great director like Scorsese or Spielberg, to see the artist and individually create something with the artist that is different from what he would create for another artist. A lot of producers try to put their sound onto you, whereas Pharrell really creates something individual for the artist."

Thicke explained that his and Pharrell's goofing around in the studio led to them behaving in a mock predatory fashion. "We started acting like we were two old men on a porch hollering at girls like, 'Hey, where you going, girl? Come over here!'" he said. He also clarified to *Billboard* the meaning of the song's title, saying it referred to "the good-girl/bad-girl thing and what's appropriate".

"It's about what's right and what's wrong and what's inappropriate and appropriate," he expanded. "I'm semi-existential and realistic."

Critical responses to the song were mostly positive – like the song's rise up the charts, negative reactions were slow in coming at first. *The Michigan Daily*'s Jackson Howard gave it an 'A' grade and praised it as "one of Pharrell's best beats in years ... by the time the multilayered and carnal harmonies of the chorus come in, the song is completely on fire." *Billboard*'s Chris Payne compared it to Justin Timberlake's 2013 single 'Suit & Tie' and called it a "bubbly bit of disco-shuffling R&B". Digital Spy's Lewis Corner, who gave the song three out of five stars, tentatively picked up on the racy content and remarked: "It's a subject that, when in the right hands, can be smooth and soulful, but in the wrong, crass and chauvinistic... You need the right balance of charm and swagger to pull it off." *The Village Voice*'s Pazz & Jop annual critics' poll, meanwhile, ranked 'Blurred Lines' at number four in a songs of the year list, tied with Kanye West's 'New Slaves'. It was left to Rob Sheffield of *Rolling Stone* to sum up the loathing felt by many towards it, naming it "The Worst Song of This or Any Other Year".

It took a while for the video's imagery to seep into people's consciousness, perhaps because they were duped at first by the proposition made by Pharrell that it was really an exploration of the rights and wrongs of courtship. It was directed by Diane Martel, also the director of Miley Cyrus' notorious 'We Can't Stop' video (2013). She had worked with Pharrell before, on another contentious promo, for N★E★R★D's 'Lapdance' in 2001, which featured topless or semi-clad females (depending on which version you watched, whether the "clean" or unexpurgated video) cavorting over Williams and fellow N★E★R★Ds Chad Hugo and Shay Haley.

The intention this time was to capture some of 'Lapdance''s excitement and licentious atmosphere, to create a fuss and draw attention to the record. The single's steady ascent up the charts was helped not a little by the video, which caught on arguably quicker than the song and gave it an extra notoriety.

"We had an artist that had never had a hit on radio. It was a non-traditional song; it didn't sound like a Timbaland or Benny Blanco record. So we had to approach the market in an interesting way," offered Jordan Feldstein, Thicke's manager. He decided a viral video, with its attendant outrage – as outfits from The Sex Pistols to Frankie Goes To Hollywood could attest – was the best way to achieve this.

"The idea behind the 'Blurred Lines' video was to make a great viral piece – and it worked," continued Feldstein. "Without the initiative it took for Robin and me to put that piece together, he would not be having the level of success right now. I knew it would get it banned quickly... Getting something banned actually helps you. Since then it has just been on a rocketship upwards."

Feldstein explained that the concept, such as it was, was Martel's. In the video, filmed at Mack Sennett Studios in Silver Lake, Thicke, T.I. and Pharrell are caught casually standing in front of a light-pink backdrop as they mug at the camera and flirt with models Emily Ratajkowski, Elle Evans and Jessi M'Bengue, who pose and dance, sashay and strut. On screen, at various intervals, the hashtag "#THICKE" flashes, as does the legend, "ROBIN THICKE HAS A BIG DICK" spelled out in silver balloons. In the "unrated" version of the video, the models are topless and wear skin-coloured G-strings. In the "censored" version, they are scantily clad and the hashtag is #BLURREDLINES.

The unrated version of the video was removed from YouTube after just under a week because of its nude content, although by July it had been restored and has since generated almost 70 million views on website Vevo. Its very raciness – not least because of the presence of three topless women – was the cause of its popularity. Thicke attributed the brief ban to national prudishness.

"That's just America," he said, dismissively. "I definitely don't have any problem with nudity. I think people that are uncomfortable in their own bodies or are uncomfortable with their own bodies don't want to see other peoples'."

In a way, the video to 'Blurred Lines' was designed as one big wind-up, to see how far Thicke, Pharrell and T.I. could go. "We tried to do everything that was taboo," teased Thicke, alluding to the animals, giant syringes, gimp masks and general air of seedy chauvinism in the video. "Bestiality, drug injections, and everything that is completely derogatory towards women. Because all three of us are happily married with children, we were like, 'We're the perfect guys to make fun of this.' People say, 'Hey, do you think this is degrading to women?' I'm like, 'Of course it is. What a pleasure it is to degrade a woman. I've never gotten to do that before. I've always respected women.'"

Later, Thicke told Oprah Winfrey that he was being ironic, describing the above quotation from *GQ* as a "bad joke", clarifying that the interview was taken entirely out of context and made mention of the fact that, while he was saying what he did, he was doing an impression of comedian Will Ferrell playing the character of Ron Burgundy.

Thicke was less playful and more direct in another interview, in which he tried to offer a justification for its imagery and content. "The video breaks all the rules," he said. "Everything you're not supposed to do in a video we did. I think it's just resonating to everybody that it's fun, it's sexy and it's cool and that's hard to find. Most of the time big pop songs are very corny. Even though you love them, they're guilty pleasures. This one doesn't feel so guilty."

It was also an attempt to counter the overtly serious nature of his previous videos, which were "about love and pride and relationships and hope and getting over insecurities and vulnerabilities". This was just him, he insisted, having fun; just three married dads reliving their misspent youths. "At first it was me and Pharrell," Thicke told GQ. "Then I thought, who else is a grown Southern gentleman with a family? T.I. Even though he's a hardcore rapper, he's a real Southern gentleman. He says 'Sir' and 'Ma'am', he stays cool, and he's really beloved. Pharrell's the same way. It was just three really nice guys having a good time together."

And openly, innocently, appreciating women's bodies. "We just wanted to turn it over on its head and make people go, 'Women and their bodies are beautiful. Men are always gonna want to follow them around.'"

Thicke recalled that, following the video's early ban, his wife, actress Paula Patton, tweeted: "Violence is ugly. Nudity is beautiful. And the 'Blurred Lines' video makes me wanna..." With all the world's problems, he argued: "Nudity should not be the issue."

And yet an issue is exactly what it became. *The Wall Street Journal*'s Elly Brinkley, considering the video, the sight of the topless models dancing with the fully clothed Thicke, Williams and T.I., the lyric of the song, particularly the "I know you want it" refrain, and using the word popular among young third-wave feminists, asked the question: "Is Robin Thicke's 'Blurred Lines' a 'rapey' song?" A BBC reporter, equally exercised, suggested to Thicke that 'Blurred Lines' "promoted rape", and he replied that he didn't want to "dignify that with a response. That's ridiculous". Thicke also defended the video in an August interview with the Associated Press, saying, "For all the controversy and all this other stuff that people try to make it seem like that's more important, what's really important about music and entertainment is to entertain and make people feel good." He added that 'Blurred Lines' was "a feminist movement in itself".

The main problem for Brinkley and others was that the song seemed to undermine the importance of consent in sexual relationships. "The very title of the song draws from the rhetoric of rape apologists who believe that date rape isn't real rape and that sexual assault is often a 'grey area'," wrote Brinkley.

British newspaper *The Independent* ran an article condemning the track, pointing out the lyric "Nothing like your last guy/ He don't smack that ass and pull your hair like that" and confirming that 'Blurred Lines' had been "criticised by a UK rape charity and online commentators for trivialising sexual violence, objectifying women and reinforcing rape myths". Katie Russell, a spokeswoman for Rape Crisis, a charity raising awareness and understanding of sexual violence, protested that the lyrics to 'Blurred Lines' seemed "to glamorise violence against women".

"Both the lyrics and the video seem to objectify and degrade women, using misogynistic language and imagery that many people would find not only distasteful or offensive but also really quite old-fashioned," she said. She added that the song reinforced the idea among certain sectors of society that provocatively dressed women, or women who don't explicitly refuse sexual advances, are "blurring lines" for men.

"More disturbingly," Russell furthered, alluding to the notion of "blurred lines", "certain lyrics are explicitly sexually violent and appear to reinforce victim-blaming rape myths, for example about women giving 'mixed signals' through their dress or behaviour, saying 'no' when they really mean 'yes' and so on."

Feminist websites around the world were unanimous in their criticism of the song and video and saw them as an incitement to degrade women. Feminist blog The Vagenda branded the video "generally an orgy of female objectification", while The Daily Beast's Tricia Romanumber criticised the single as "kind of rapey". Referring to the song's refrain, "I know you want it", Romanumber said: "Call me a cynic, but that phrase does not exactly encompass the notion of consent in sexual activity... Seriously, this song is disgusting – though admittedly very catchy." JH, a Vagenda blogger, wrote: "Thicke and Pharrell probably genuinely think that this video is empowering for women. And the women in the video probably feel like they are being cool and rebellious by doing it. However, the only real irony is when Thicke sings "[I] tried to domesticate you/But you're an animal, baby, it's in your nature", because the whole video is about domestication. It is not about girls exposing their bodies for their own amusement but for Thicke's."

An article in *The Guardian* described 'Blurred Lines' and the sexual-political furore surrounding it as "the latest development in the story of how the biggest song of the year became the most controversial of the decade". Journalist Dorian Lynskey recounted that, in September 2013, contributors to Project Unbreakable, a photographic project dedicated to rape survivors, held up placards comparing words spoken by their attackers to lines from the song. That same month, Edinburgh University Students' Association (EUSA) became the first student body to ban 'Blurred Lines'.

"It promotes a very worrying attitude towards sex and consent," explained Kirsty Haigh, EUSA's vice-president of services. "This is about ensuring that everyone is fully aware that you need enthusiastic consent before sex. The song says: 'You know you want it.' Well, you can't know they want it unless they tell you they want it."

Lynskey argued that 'Blurred Lines' was "part of a bigger debate about the messages of pop lyrics and videos", citing other examples when Thicke, "like a sex-pest Zelig", appeared, such as at Miley Cyrus' performance at the Video Music Awards in August, a cameo that "ignited another firestorm of indignation on several fronts".

There were oppositional voices in the debate, or at least some who considered 'Blurred Lines' to be merely sexist pop business as usual. The implication from these quarters was that Thicke – and he seemed to be the object of most if not all of the opprobrium, rather than T.I. or Pharrell – was being largely singled out because of his seeming oleaginous smarminess.

"It really did boggle my mind when people started freaking out about it," declared US music critic Maura Johnston. "This is just a cheesy pickup line song and everyone was like: 'No, it's about forcing a woman against her will.' There are so many songs out there that are worse about demeaning women. Maybe it's an easy target because Robin Thicke is kind of slimy. Right now there's a lot of tension between women and men online so this was a way of women taking a piece of pop culture and saying: 'No, we're against this.' But it's weird to me because I didn't see it and I still don't."

There was another defender of the video, who also happened to be female: Diane Martel, the director of 'Blurred Lines'. As Dorian Lynskey pointed out, the assumption was that Martel was barely present at the video, while the men were calling the shots, whereas had it been a male director all the vitriol would have been poured on him and he would have been blamed for it all.

Commentators had been all but ignoring Martel's defence of her work – and balancing statements from Pharrell, who reminded everyone that "that treatment was written and shot by a female director, who's a feminist" – so keen were they to crucify the male participants.

"It forces the men to feel playful and not at all like predators," Martel told US website Grantland of her approach to 'Blurred Lines', positing the original idea that, if anything, it was demeaning towards the men. "I directed the girls to look into the camera. This is very intentional and they do it most of the time; they are in the power position. I don't think the video is sexist. The lyrics are ridiculous; the guys are silly as fuck."

Thicke defended the video in an interview with BBC's *Newsbeat* at 1Xtra Live in Liverpool, saying, "I don't think people got it", and explaining that he wrote the song for his wife, Paula Patton. In the song, he croons "she's my good girl" – this was, he claimed, a compliment towards Patton, who the 36-year-old began dating in high school, when they were both in their mid-teens. "She's my good girl," he said. "And I know she wants it because we've been together for 20 years."

Thicke's father – 66-year-old actor Alan Thicke, best known for his role as Dr Jason Seaver in US sitcom *Growing Pains* during the eighties and early nineties – weighed into the debate, declaring: "He's a wonderful son and a great artist."

He mused at considerable length: "I think that there are blurred lines within the 'Blurred Lines'. T.I.'s rap is kind of graphic; Robin's point of view, I think, in his own parts of the song... is kind of female empowerment when you look at it. It's not so much 'we know you want it' – it's 'we hope you want it'. It's still a guy waiting for permission, saying, 'I'm not your maker'. Nobody grabs anybody; we're waiting for permission here. And not only that, but it's guys trying to be cute and funny.

"This is not a lascivious video," he added. "There's no humping and grinding, as we've been seeing in music videos for two decades now... I'm actually a little surprised at the response, at least to the nudity, because I've seen things I thought were much more sexual than simply [being] topless. If it was that simple to get global attention and create this maelstrom over simply taking your top off, hell, somebody should have done that long ago. Most of the other videos for years have been about booty... For some reason, when they switched from booty to booby, everyone went nuts."

In an interview with *The Independent*'s Saturday arts magazine *Radar*, Pharrell rallied round, claiming that the lyrics to 'Blurred Lines' came from "a decent place". He even went so far as to declare that the song was about rejection and a man's inability to get the woman he wants, not anything as offensive as sex and rape.

"I'd never want to say anything about sex," he smarted. "Like, 'rapey' would mean, 'I'm gonna do this to you, you know you want me to do that to you...' You have to make sure that you're coming from a decent place. And I was coming from a decent place. Because when you look at the song in totality you realise that the song's about a woman who wanted to... who felt something, but decided to take it out on the dance floor."

Williams insisted there was nothing wrong with lyrics such as "I know you want it", which he said referred to a male fantasy about a strong female who rejects him. "What's wrong with that? I know I want it," he said. "The song was a pie-in-the-sky idea of a conversation that never took place! The song ain't about doing it! Nothing ever happens. 'Cause she's a good girl. Duh!"

Asked by listings magazine *Time Out* whether "sexy videos are sexist", backed into a corner, Pharrell's response was somewhat fantastical. "Is it sexist when you walk around in a museum and a lot of the statues have their boobs out?" he wondered aloud. "The women in that video weren't doing anything sexual: they were only dancing. Just because they had their boobs out, that was 'sexist'. I didn't do anything sexually suggestive to any of those women, I wouldn't allow it. I have respect and I know the message that I want to put out. I'm a fun guy."

Furthermore, he said, some of his best friends – and relatives – are female. His mother, even, is one. "Look, I love [women], because I know their importance," he said. "If women wanted to shut down this country, economically, they could just not go to work and the UK would be finished. If they wanted to kill off our species, they'd just decide not to have babies. And there's going to be a huge shift, a huge shift. There will be a time when women get paid as much as men. There will be a time when, like, 75 percent of our world leaders will be women. All the presidents and prime ministers. There will come a time. And I'm going to be on the right side of that shift when it happens…

"I want to support women," he added, with a flash of his irresistible grin, "but that doesn't mean I won't make another song where girls' behinds are everywhere."

Speaking to Howard Stern, Pharrell explained that 'Blurred Lines' was almost not a hit, complaining that the record company prevaricated about releasing it as a single, sitting on it for eight months. He compared the excitement he felt at the track to the feeling he had when he completed work on Nelly's 'Hot In Herre'.

"Nelly and I were jumping around in the room for that one," he recalled. "Same with 'Blurred Lines'. Robin and I got it. My managers got it. Robin Thicke's managers didn't originally. It was only when I said I was going to cover it myself for the *Despicable Me* soundtrack that they snapped into action and agreed to Robin Thicke doing it."

Pharrell admitted to Stern that it was the video that "put it on the map", stressing that it was an "incredibly accomplished", 51-year-old female director who came up with the treatment and filmed it. "The chick in the video," said Stern, provocatively, "was incredibly hot."

Pharrell laughed. Stern continued: "Did you, during the making of the video, think, 'This is kind of crazy, we've got a naked girl dancing in front of us?' Did you think it was incredibly sexist?"

"No!" Pharrell snapped. "There are always naked women. I basically did a lot of dancing and enjoyed it."

He revealed that he got the idea for the song "from a friend, a girl who was having a bit of a tough time". Their conversation really affected him.

"It struck me: a good girl has bad thoughts just like a bad person has good thoughts," he told the radio host. "I was trying to tear down the categorical walls of society and their expectations. Let's write a song where the good girl has bad thoughts, but she's not going to do anything bad, she's going to take it out on the dance floor. And that's what I did."

So instead of being misogynistic, the song was actually Pharrell being misunderstood? He agreed that this was the case. Stern then wondered why he gave the song to Thicke, instead of singing it himself?

"Because," he replied, "he immediately came in and started grooving to it. He understood it. Robin is a masterful, masterful singer. And performer and musician. Go see him – he is a beast onstage."

Ever prolific and able to juggle several jobs at once, Williams told Stern that, while he was working on 'Blurred Lines' in one recording studio, he had Miley Cyrus in another, where they were putting the finishing touches to country-funk hoedown '4x4'.

Did his collaborators, worried Stern, ever get possessive? "Sometimes," conceded Pharrell. "And then, after the first song, they understand why I do it. It's like when you're smelling fragrances, they give you coffee beans to refresh the olfactory palate."

With all the controversy surrounding 'Blurred Lines', would he, Stern wondered, work with Robin Thicke again? "Absolutely," he replied.

But there was more controversy to come for Pharrell as a result of his team-up with Thicke. In August 2013, Thicke, Williams, and Harris (T.I.) sued the family of the song's composer, Marvin Gaye, and music publishers Bridgeport Music, for a "declaratory judgement" that 'Blurred Lines' did not infringe copyrights of the defendants. This was a pre-emptive move based on an earlier accusation by Gaye's family that the song's writers had copied the "feel" and "sound" of Gaye's 1977 hit – they feared the Gayes would be litigious, and sought to affirm that 'Blurred Lines' was "strikingly different" to 'Got To Give It Up'. Additionally, Bridgeport claimed that the song illegally sampled 'Sexy Ways', a 1974 track by George Clinton's psychedelic funk band Funkadelic.

Pharrell responded to the lawsuit by contending that 'Blurred Lines' and 'Got To Give It Up' were "completely different" and that they were in different keys, the one minor and the other major. A member of rap troupe A Tribe Called Quest – Ahmir Khalib Thompson, known as Questlove – even sprang to his defence, agreeing that it was derivative but positing 'Blurred Lines' as an example not of plagiarism but of homage.

On October 30, 2014, a California judge ruled that the Gaye family's lawsuit against Thicke and Williams could proceed, stating the plaintiffs had "made a sufficient showing that elements of 'Blurred Lines' may be substantially similar to protected, original elements of 'Got To Give It Up'." The trial began on February 10, 2015, although Williams and Thicke managed to have it agreed in court that Gaye's track would not be played during the trial, mainly because this was an argument about the sheet music for the song and no other musical elements. The judge commented, "I don't expect Marvin Gaye's voice to be part of this case."

The trial focused on detailed analyses of the technical, on-paper matter of chords and notes in both 'Blurred Lines' and 'Got To Give It Up'. Williams spent more than an hour describing his musical process and how he came to write 'Blurred Lines'. Though he admitted a similarity between his and Gaye's song, he insisted the latter never entered his head while writing his track; rather, he said, he was "channelling... that late seventies feeling".

As for Thicke, in court he performed a medley of songs – by artists including U2, Bob Marley and The Beatles – to prove how many tracks do have chords and melodies in common without necessarily copying one another. In a bid to distance himself from the fracas, Thicke then testified that he wasn't present when the song was written, despite receiving credit. Instead, it was Pharrell Williams who wrote the majority of the song after Thicke confessed to being "high on Vicodin and alcohol when [he] showed up at the studio".

"The biggest hit of my career was written and produced by someone else, and I was jealous and I wanted some credit," he said in a statement. As a result, the composition – "the beat and ... almost every single part of the song" – was Williams' alone. Pharrell admitted, too, that he was "in the driver's seat" during the song's creation and agreed that Thicke's contributions to the process had been "embellished".

A month later, on March 10, a jury found Thicke and Williams liable for copyright infringement, but not T.I. The unanimous jury ordered that the pair should pay Gaye's three children – Nona, Frankie and Marvin Gaye III, who inherited the copyright to the soul legend's music following his death in 1984 – $7.4 million (£4.8 million) in damages for copyright infringement ('Blurred

Lines' earned $16 million, or £11 million, in profits, making $5 million – £3 million – each for Thicke and Williams).

"It is our wish that our dad's legacy, and all great music, past, present, and future, be enjoyed and protected, with the knowledge that adhering to copyright standards assures our musical treasures will always be valued," they said in a statement. Gaye's daughter, Nona, wept as the verdict was being read and was hugged by her attorney, Richard Busch, who added outside of court that, "They fought this fight despite every odd being against them".

"Right now, I feel free," an emotional Nona Gaye said after the verdict. "Free from... Pharrell Williams and Robin Thicke's chains and what they tried to keep on us and the lies that were told."

There followed an open letter "from the children of Marvin Gaye" in which they stated that their father would have supported their decision to seek justice in the 'Blurred Lines' trial. "If he were alive today, we feel he would embrace the technology available to artists and the diverse music choices and spaces accessible to fans who can stream a song at a moment's notice," the Gaye offspring wrote. "But we also know he would be vigilant about safeguarding the artist's rights. He also gave credit where credit is due."

The Gaye family proceeded to send a warning shot across the bows of any recording artist intending to seek inspiration from soul or pop's rich catalogue, declaring that, "With the digital age upon us, the threat of greater infringement looms for every artist".

Busch branded Williams and Thicke "liars" who went beyond trying to emulate the sound of Gaye's late seventies music and copied the song outright.

As for Thicke and Williams, they immediately announced their intention to appeal the verdict. In a statement following the trial, their lawyer Howard King said, "There was no properly admissible evidence upon which the jury could have found copying." He commented that the decision in favour of Gaye's heirs "could have a chilling effect on musicians who try to emulate an era or another artist's sound", not to mention the possible tarnishing of Williams' career and legacy that could ensue.

"This case is far from over," King warned, denying there were any substantial similarities between 'Blurred Lines' and the sheet music the Gayes submitted to obtain copyright protection. He described the jury verdict against Williams and Thicke as "an abject miscarriage of justice, unsupported by the evidence and contrary to the law".

Following the verdict, an attorney for Pharrell and Thicke told *Rolling Stone*, "They're firm, rock solid, in the conclusion that they wrote this song independently from the heart and soul with no input from anyone, Marvin Gaye or anyone else. They sleep well knowing they didn't copy the song."

There was, however, further trouble for Williams when Gaye's family subsequently moved to block future sales of 'Blurred Lines'. They claimed that the jury's decision covered only past sales of the song and did not award the Gayes a revenue percentage going forward. They even called for the verdict to be amended to include T.I., who contributed a verse to the song and in doing so theoretically owed some royalties of his own, as well as the relevant record labels: Universal Music, Interscope Records and Star Trek Entertainment.

Understandably, with so much at stake, there was much heated debate in the wake of the ruling. Nile Rodgers was nonplussed by the verdict, decreeing the two songs entirely dissimilar pieces of work. "Compositionally, purely compositionally, I don't think they should have lost that case," he said of Williams and Thicke, a generous assessment considering the number of artists who had "borrowed" the tune, beat and bassline of 'Good Times' among other Chic hits. "'Got To Give It Up' is clearly a blues structure; 'Blurred Lines' isn't at all."

Williams himself finally spoke about the judge's ruling after the court case. "The verdict handicaps any creator out there who is making something that might be inspired by something else," he told *The Financial Times*. "This applies to fashion, music, design… anything. If we lose our freedom to be inspired, we're going to look up one day and the entertainment industry as we know it will be frozen in litigation. This is about protecting the intellectual rights of people who have ideas.

"Everything that's around you in a room was inspired by something or someone," he added. "If you kill that, there's no creativity."

In the *Financial Times'* article, which assessed the impact of the 'Blurred Lines' case on the entertainment industry as a whole, producer Harvey Weinstein argued that, in today's climate, Andy Warhol or Roy Lichtenstein – two artists directly inspired by pop cultural artefacts past and present – would not be able to create without fear of the legal ramifications.

Appearing on Howard Stern's radio show after the court case, Williams was asked whether he was shocked to have had the lawsuit issued against him. "Of course," he replied. "It disappointed me because I'm such a huge fan of his."

He added that stars of the stature of Elton John and Stevie Wonder had all spoken out in his defence, declaring on their behalf that "you can't copyright a sound, feel or genre."

"You can only copyright musical notation," he added, which is why he was so keen for Gaye's family and the prosecution to, as he urged, "Look at the sheet music!"

If it had been Pharrell's only song, 'Blurred Lines' might have provided the full stop to a brief but illustrious career. Actually, popular as it was, it was just one of many of his successes. And he was hardly about to allow its notoriety to derail him. In fact, unbelievable as it seemed given the magnitude of its sales, notoriety and ubiquity, it was about to be eclipsed by another of his records, one that would make 'Blurred Lines' look like a commercial non-starter.

CHAPTER 10

Happy Ending

"I never expected in a million, kajillion years that anyone would want to hear what I have to sell in terms of a body of work"
— Pharrell Williams

If the 'Blurred Lines' court case weighed heavily on Pharrell, he didn't show it. This was perhaps because of the stability and comfort provided by his home life. On Saturday October 12, 2013, he married his longtime girlfriend, Helen Lasichanh, a former star volleyball player at St. Thomas University in Miami as well as a model and designer who had been featured in the *Huffington Post* and *NY Post* for her fashion sense. The couple already had a son, Rocket Ayer Williams, who was born in November 2008 – the musician has described him as "the best song that I've ever co-written". He discussed the child with Howard Stern in 2014. "No, he's a sweet boy," he told the radio host, who had asked whether the boy was "a pain in the ass". On the contrary, Williams described him as highly musical – "He's been playing chords since he was four," he said. He also explained the derivation of his name:

it was from songs by some of his favourite musicians such as Elton John ('Rocket Man'), Stevie Wonder ('Rocket Love') and Herbie Hancock ('Rockit'). "A rocket is a man-made machine meant to ascend," he added.

Pharrell and his new bride became engaged in 2012 (although she wasn't spotted publicly with her new diamond ring until July 16, 2013, at the premiere of Batman movie *The Dark Knight Rises*). They exchanged vows in Miami, Florida, in front of a variety of famous friends, including Usher, Busta Rhymes, Jay-Z, Justin Timberlake, Gwen Stefani and Robin Thicke and his then wife, actress Paula Patton. The ceremony took place at the Kampong National Tropical Botanical Gardens in Coconut Grove. The photographer for the event was the feted Terry Richardson, and Lasichanh wore a navy blue and green checked gown instead of a traditional white wedding dress.

According to a source, Usher and Busta Rhymes performed a mini-concert at the wedding, and several of Williams' hits were played, all of which helped make it "the most fun wedding I've ever been to". The couple posed for photos onboard a yacht called *Never Say Never*.

Pharrell was effusive about family life in the wake of his marriage. "It's awesome," he said, adding that he was reluctant to offer anyone relationship advice but that, for anyone considering wedlock, it would, he suggested, be wise to ensure deep friendship first and foremost. Marry your "bestie", he urged, and in that way, "Y'all agree on everything, and every night is like a sleepover," he told host Savannah Guthrie on America's *The Today Show*.

It could have been so different for Pharrell, had the superstar carried on misbehaving. He used to cheat on his many former girlfriends. "You've had some crazy experiences," Howard Stern said to the erstwhile lothario, commenting that he had "read somewhere" that Pharrell had "made love to eight women at once", to which his co-host Robin Quivers exclaimed: "What? How do you do that? That's physically impossible!"

"It is physically impossible," replied Pharrell, unruffled by the personal nature of the enquiries. "What it meant was one at a time."

"Where were you when you did this?" asked Stern.

"Out of my mind!" quipped Williams.

Was he, wondered Stern, alluding to his drug intake, "on anything" at the time?

"No," he said. "I wasn't on anything. At that time it was just the girls – that was my vice. How many years ago was it? Over 10 years ago."

Now, he insisted, having met Lasichanh, he had been forced to change his ways. Unexpectedly, given his irresistibility and attraction to the opposite sex, she didn't immediately fall for his charms as she was already involved with someone else. It was a wake-up call for Pharrell.

In an interview with Oprah Winfrey, he recalled, "She didn't answer half of my text messages [at first]. Egotistically, no [that didn't intrigue me]. I was like, 'Oh yeah?' because I had that kind of money and because I had that kind of reach, I thought I was entitled and I had learned that no, she has a boyfriend and she's not interested."

Williams was forced to settle with just being friends for two-and-a-half years until Lasichanh became single again, but he confessed his immaturity almost cost him her love.

"I hurt her a lot in the very beginning once she was free and was available, because I had given her all of this attention but I wasn't ready to, like, let go [of bachelor life]," he explained. "I looked at my life and I was like, 'Man, I could keep doing this for another 10 years, is that what I want to do?' And so I made a decision. And then we made a decision and just started dating."

Another happy event, and match made in heaven, came in January 2014, when Pharrell, Nile Rodgers, Daft Punk and Stevie Wonder performed 'Get Lucky' together onstage at the 56th Annual Grammy Awards in LA, where the song won awards for Record of the Year and Best Pop Duo/Group Performance. After Williams and Wonder each had their turn at verses of the hit, Daft Punk – dressed in pristine white helmets and suits for their first appearance on national TV in six years – were revealed behind the glass of the makeshift recording studio set, a high-budget studio, evoking images of the milieu that brought their album *Random Access Memories* to life. There followed a flawless transition into a medley of some of the stars' best-known songs: Chic's 'Le Freak', Wonder's 'Another Star', and snippets of Daft Punk's 'Harder, Better, Faster, Stronger'.

Watching the stellar performance at the Staples Center were numerous celebrity attendees: Katy Perry, Paul McCartney, Beyoncé, Jay-Z, Ringo Starr, Yoko Ono, Bruno Mars, Steven Tyler of Aerosmith and John Legend.

Earlier in the evening, Daft Punk took to the stage to accept their award – presented by no lesser a personage than Smokey Robinson – although neither of them spoke, instead allowing Williams to do so.

"On behalf of the robots," he began after Daft Punk gestured for him to walk up to the mic. After thanking the Recording Academy and the other nominees, Williams said, on behalf of Daft Punk: "Of course, they want to thank their families," prompting laughter from the star-studded audience.

Following the performance, Rodgers enthused about sharing the stage with Wonder. "Normally, I'm not at a loss for words, but this is a shock for me tonight. Getting a chance to play with Stevie Wonder was all I expected. I'm really blown away," he said in the press room.

At the end of the nearly four-hour show, Daft Punk took home the night's biggest prize, for Album of the Year. The robot duo embraced each other, leading to several hashtags on Twitter, including #RobotHug. There was another pop-culture moment after the show when Williams' Vivienne Westwood-designed mountie hat – a tall, wide-brimmed affair that *Billboard* described as looking like "something between a Rocky and Bullwinkle Mountie and a condom" – became a Photoshop meme and earned its own Twitter and Instagram accounts.

There was another Pharrell hat moment in June 2014 when he was featured on the cover of UK *Elle* wearing a Native American war bonnet. It triggered a #NotHappy Twitter campaign. Williams apologised for posing in the feather headdress. "I am genuinely sorry," he wrote in a statement provided to Buzzfeed, although the apology was not reprinted on his official website, Facebook or Twitter accounts. "I respect and honour every kind of race, background and culture."

Supporters of the South Dakota Indian reservations called for a boycott of *Elle* on their Facebook page. "Our Culture is not an accessory!" wrote Monika Trujillo. Gail Lichtsinn underlined the traditional function of Williams' headgear: "Those headdresses are earned and not worn to make a buck or draw attention. They have meaning and are worn by our men with pride and dignity."

Williams stated that he had some Native American ancestry. This, argued the Indian Country Today Media Network, "doesn't matter". In an article in *The Guardian*, Sean Michaels reported the ICTMN's words on the subject: that the eagle-feather war bonnet was not a wacky fashion addition but a sacred ceremonial item, one "earned over the course of one's lifetime" and used by only 12 of the United States' 562 federally recognised tribes.

Still, any controversy that arose in 2014 was fairly comprehensively trounced by the all-encompassing success of 'Happy'.

'Happy' was written, produced and performed by Pharrell, with backing vocals by Rhea Dummett, Trevon Henderson, Ashley L. Lee, Shamika Hightower, Jasmine Murray and Terrence Rolleand. It was taken from the soundtrack album to cartoon comedy *Despicable Me 2*, which went on general release the summer before. It was also the lead single from Williams' second studio album, *G I R L*, issued in March 2014.

The single, later nominated for an Academy Award for Best Original Song, was a super-ebullient piece of sixties-referencing pop (a mood of giddy euphoria captured most effectively by the lyric, "Clap along if you feel like a room without a roof"). It boasted a spare arrangement including programmed drums, a bass and keyboard part, and handclaps both programmed and played. Pharrell had apparently attempted to finish the song numerous times before getting it right.

"It was actually nine versions before I got to the tenth," he told US talk show *Good Morning America*. "I got to point zero, and I just said to myself, 'How do you make a song about a guy who is so happy and relentless in doing so?' That's when I realised that the answer had been sleeping in the question all along."

There were shades of Motown in the rhythm and of Curtis Mayfield in the falsetto – ominously, Marvin Gaye's children noted, in the wake of the 'Blurred Lines' court case, some similarities between their father's song 'Ain't That Peculiar' and 'Happy', although as *Rolling Stone* pointed out, "The family has confirmed [in an open letter] that they 'have absolutely no claim whatsoever concerning 'Happy'."

It was first released on November 21, 2013, accompanied by an award-winning video (Best Music Video at the 57th Annual Grammy Awards) in which Pharrell and a cast of dozens – including Earl Sweatshirt, Tyler, The Creator, comedy actor Steve Carell (one of the stars of *Despicable Me 2*) and basketball legend

Magic Johnson – dance gleefully in a variety of settings around Los Angeles. The video – the official four-minute edit – had, by April 2015, 631 million views on YouTube.

There was also a full, unexpurgated, ground-breaking interactive version of the video – the world's first 24-hour video. It was filmed – all one takes – using 400 dancing extras with a Steadicam across eight miles of LA over the course of 11 days.

"It's been 30 years since [Michael Jackson's John Landis-directed video for] 'Thriller' first showed us how ambitious a pop promo could be, and it's good to see innovation is still the name of the game, even if it's more an outlandish gimmick than something you'd want to watch over and over," wrote British music paper *NME*, which commissioned one of its journalists to watch the video in its entirety. Website Pitchfork offered its own take on the video, with an article entitled "5 Best Things To Watch In Pharrell's 24-Hour Music Video". For the record, they chose a gas station B-Boy doing a series of Michael Jackson "crotch-grab shuffles"; Magic Johnson "dancing in his private trophy room"; Jamie Foxx "using his adorable daughter as a prop", a "goofy cameo" in which Tyler, The Creator, Earl Sweatshirt and Jasper Dolphin of Odd Future "do a Broadway-dandy dance routine that finds them twirl-jumping into jazz-handed layouts every time they hear the word 'happy'"; and Pharrell's final cameo (he appears 24 times, once at the start of each hour) in which the singer, still looking delirious, "has a dance-off with a little girl that ends in the most charismatic high-five you've ever seen".

Pitchfork concluded that, after 24-hours' worth of ribbon dancers and riverdancers, skateboarders, park rangers and swing-dancing coeds, the video served as "a visual census of a place, an homage to the neighbourhoods of Los Angeles and the people who live there".

Needless to say, the song itself fared exceptionally well. It reached number one in the US, the UK, Canada, Ireland, New

Zealand, and 19 other countries. It was the best-selling single of 2014 in the US with 6.45 million units shifted, and in the UK, where 1.5 million were sold (and where it spent 70 weeks in the Top 75). In fact, worldwide, it sold 14 million copies, making it the planet's most popular song that year (in April 2015 it was announced that 'Happy' was also 2014's most downloaded song globally).

'Happy' was Pharrell's first release for Columbia. In a December 2013 press release, Rob Stringer, the chairman of Columbia Records, declared: "When we excitedly partnered with Pharrell in January of this year, we felt it was his time again. Since then, 'Blurred Lines' and 'Get Lucky' have defined pop music in 2013, and now we are preparing to launch Pharrell as a global solo superstar in 2014. 'Happy' is just the beginning."

'Happy', like so many of Williams' songs, had originally been written with someone else in mind – on this occasion, CeeLo Green. Indeed, the latter recorded a version of it, one that Williams considered superior to his own, but Elektra Records, Green's record label, decided against its signing releasing it since he was on the verge of releasing his Christmas album, *CeeLo's Magic Moment*.

"CeeLo did a version of it," Pharrell admitted to Howard Stern. "It burns my version! It's way better," he said, adding that the movie company behind *Despicable Me 2* had also insisted that Pharrell's version be the released one. Nevertheless, he proceeded with the notion that CeeLo's record company was behind the decision.

"How do I say this diplomatically?" he deadpanned. "The powers that be at that time did not see it fit for him."

Was CeeLo, goaded Stern, now feeling suicidal, given the song's enormous worldwide success? "No," deflected Williams. "He was one of the most gracious people about it. He congratulated me when it came out. He's a super-stand-up guy. A tremendous talent."

As Pharrell saw it, he was a glorified backroom boy who lucked out by acquiring a second career as a frontman. "I can't believe it's become what it is," he said of his career. "I'm honoured. As a producer and a writer, I never expected in a million, kajillion years that anyone would want to hear what I have to sell in terms of a body of work."

There were some blips in an otherwise distinctly joyous period for Pharrell. The *Daily Mail* reported that a 32-year-old North Carolina woman – Courtney Sanford, of High Point – had died after crashing her car head-on into a recycling truck while posting selfies and a Facebook update about how happy she was while listening to the Pharrell song. The last words Sanford shared with her friends online were: "The happy song makes me HAPPY."

"In a matter of seconds, a life was over just so she could notify some friends that she was happy," a police spokesperson said.

"It definitely bothered me," Pharrell said of the incident.

Pharrell's ode to joy found itself inadvertently the cause of more unpleasantness when the video became viral in Albania and caused controversy over the use of images of Albanian former dictator Enver Hoxha. More seriously still, six Iranian singers – three men and three unveiled women – were arrested for appearing in a viral video dancing to the song in the street and on the rooftops of Tehran, mimicking the style of Pharrell's official video. They were sentenced to six months in prison and 91 lashes by the Iranian authorities, for contravening Iran's strict vulgarity laws, which prohibit public displays of dancing. They then paraded the six on state television, forcing them to express remorse for their behaviour.

The Islamic Republic condemned the video as a "vulgar clip which hurt public chastity".

Speaking shortly after the group's initial arrest, the brother of one of the video's stars told *The Telegraph* that their confessions on state television were "outrageous".

Siavash Taravati, a resident of the US, said: "The IRIB's [Islamic Republic of Iran Broadcasting] action in showing the 'confession' of my sister and her friends is just outrageous. Apparently they first arrest people without any charge or civil right to defend themselves, then interrogate them and then make them confess and finally broadcast their show."

Later the Iranian president criticised the arrest, saying in a tweet, "#Happiness is our people's right. We shouldn't be too hard on behaviours caused by joy." The dancers, along with the director of the video, were later released. And it was made clear that these were *suspended* punishments of 91 lashes each along with the jail sentences, meaning that only if another crime were to be committed in the ensuing three years would the punishments will be carried out.

Still, it was a negative outcome to what was fast becoming an anthem of universal brotherhood. Williams responded to Iran's actions on his Twitter account in May, saying: "It's beyond sad these kids were arrested for trying to spread happiness."

There were more tears to come – only these were tears of happiness – during an interview with Oprah Winfrey. The sheer enormity of Pharrell's success, and the love and devotion afforded his recent music, proved overwhelming as Winfrey played a montage of fan-created YouTube videos adapted to his number one hit, filmed in London, the Philippines, Iceland and other locations around the world.

Regarding the song, he noted how radio stations had been uninterested in the song until his film clip debuted and fan-made videos began to create attention. "It was no longer my song," he said.

Winfrey asked him about his younger days, even unearthing some childhood photos of him. "I was just thinking of your grandmother," she said, alluding to Pharrell's extraordinary popularity. "I bet she didn't even imagine that."

At this point, he began welling up.

"Why am I crying on Oprah?" he asked, rhetorically. "It's overwhelming because it's like, I love what I do and I just appreciate the fact that people have believed in me for so long that I could make it to this point, to feel *that*."

Despite the series of unfortunate events, the song had clearly brought joy to untold millions and raised the musician to a level of fame and acclaim even more elevated than the one he enjoyed in the aftermath of 'Get Lucky' and 'Blurred Lines'.

"The song has changed me," he said. "Hoisted me to heights that I've never seen before."

Was he at this point in his life, enquired Howard Stern, happy? "More so than happy," he said, "I'm grateful."

Did he ever have a bad day? "Yeah, sure," he replied, "we all do. But it could be worse."

An article in *The Guardian* examined the song's DNA from several angles, in an attempt to work out Pharrell's recipe for happiness. Andrew Fisher, head of commercial composition at University of Southampton, decided that there was something inherent in the music's composition.

"It is an elusive combination of ingredients that makes any song appeal widely, but for this song what I think helps is a very clear form and a very strong chorus hook," he said, assessing the impact of the simple verse followed by the more sophisticated chorus, "which contrasts in terms of harmony, arrangement and instrumentation".

Paddy Bickerton, professional party and wedding DJ, found it reassuringly inviting, compared to so much indie and R&B, which, he decided, "sounds weird and alien".

"'Happy' is stripped back with a good groove and a cool-sounding sixties Motown feel, so its success is down to the fact that it is pop music in its most fundamental state," he concluded, noting that, unusually for such a fast song, married couples had begun picking it as their first-dance song.

Eric Clarke, Oxford professor and author of *Music And Mind In Everyday Life*, meanwhile, picked up on the use of major chords and upbeat music in the song, and noted their association with euphoria. "Upbeat music tends to convey high energy, and one form of high energy is happiness. When most people are happy [they] tend to, in quite physiological terms, have high muscle tone; they are in an active state and are aroused," he said. "Perhaps what makes 'Happy' sound happy is that it not only has high energy, but it uses what has become a very culturally common association between major and minor in music. It uses mainly major chords which have a long history in western music as being associated with positive emotions."

Finally, George Ergatoudis, head of music for BBC Radio 1 and 1Xtra, discerned that 'Happy''s success was the result of good timing and the all-round good feelings that it invoked.

"'Happy' came out during a bleak time of year when people were feeling lower than they already were, given it was the tail end of a recession ... [People] want songs that really give them a good feeling," he mused. "The hit of elation is key to ['Happy''s] success."

Unfortunately, at the 86th Academy Awards on March 2, 2014, 'Happy' lost out on the Oscar to 'Let It Go', the theme song from Disney's computer-animated musical *Frozen*. Afterwards, when *GQ* magazine asked Williams "how badly" he wanted to win the statuette, he responded: "When they read the results, my face was... frozen. But then I thought about it, and I just decided to... let it go," he said, quoting the lyric from the Disney song.

Later that month, it was announced that Williams had been hired as the new coach for the seventh season of the American version of reality TV singing competition *The Voice*, replacing none other than CeeLo Green.

"Okay, we can OFFICIALLY say it! WE ARE SO #HAPPY to announce PHARRELL WILLIAMS = #NewVoiceCoach for SEASON 7," tweeted TV station NBC. Williams retweeted the NBC tweet, adding: "This is going to be so fun."

"It's been a huge year for Pharrell, with recognition for his contribution in the world of music – the *Despicable Me* franchise soundtracks, his Oscar-nominated song 'Happy' and his Grammy-winning collaboration with Daft Punk on the breakout dance hit 'Get Lucky'. His dominance in record sales in 2014, coupled with his incomparable accomplishments in the world of fashion and design, make him an irresistible addition to *The Voice* family," said Paul Telegdy of NBC Entertainment, pointing out that Pharrell had already done some "mentoring" on the show, making him a natural choice as full-time judge. "It is a perfect fit for *The Voice* as we evolve and reach for new heights with this franchise. It feels like we are welcoming an existing family member home."

Soon after the start of the new series of *The Voice*, however, rumours began leaking that there were behind-scenes arguments involving Pharrell and one of the other judges, Adam Levine of Maroon 5 (the remaining two judges being Gwen Stefani and country singer Blake Shelton). According to RadarOnline. com, Levine was "feeling shafted" by Williams, because he was taking all the good contestants and due to his popularity with the production staff on the show.

"Adam is just jaded after doing it for so many seasons," said a source. "Production staff are saying that not only does Adam act like an asshole, but he is totally jealous of Pharrell and this season has brought out his true colours."

In March 2014, *G I R L*, Williams' first solo album since 2006's *In My Mind*, was released. Featuring cameos by Justin Timberlake, Miley Cyrus, Daft Punk and Alicia Keys, it was his first album for Columbia in tandem with his own i am OTHER imprint, which he set up as a multimedia creative collective and record label serving as an umbrella for his Billionaire Boys Club and Ice Cream endeavours, his textile company Bionic Yarn and his dedicated YouTube channel. As for Columbia, it "made me an offer, pretty much right there at the table," he said, his agreement to the deal in no small part because he was "overwhelmed that someone wanted to know what's in my heart".

Talking about the new album, he was typically effusive. "When Columbia Records presented me with the opportunity to make an album, three things came to mind," he said. "One was the sense of overwhelming honour that I felt when I realised that they were interested in partnering with me on the album that I had always dreamt of making. Two, it would have to feel festive and urgent. And three, I instantly knew it would be called *G I R L*. I hope you like it."

This was evidently a deal whereby Pharrell would have free creative rein. Look no further than the typography of the album title, which was stylised – with capital letters and spaces between each – to add to the sense that this was more than a record, it was a statement. One early review called it a "feminist almost-concept album celebrating women and aiming to highlight society's gender imbalance".

Interviewed by Radio 1 DJ Zane Lowe backstage at the 2014 BRIT Awards, Williams specified that the capitalisation and double-spacing of the album title was deliberately designed: "Because when you look at it, it looks a little weird," he said. He added that he wished, with *G I R L*, to honour the women that had been part of his life. Clearly more affected than he seemed at the time by the negative press the single 'Blurred Lines' had received, particularly the taint of misogyny, this was his opportunity to set the record straight and clarify his position vis a vis womankind.

"There's an imbalance in society, in my opinion," he explained at the album's launch, to 100 or so representatives of the European media in the London offices of his new Sony home, "and it's going to change. A world where 75 per cent of it is run by women – that's a different world. That's gonna happen, and I want to be on the right side of it when it does."

The album opened in no uncertain terms with a flurry of strings (*The Guardian*'s Michael Cragg described it as "filmic") and a busy, hook-laden track entitled 'Marilyn Monroe', orchestrated by Williams' soundtrack associate, the Oscar-winning movie composer Hans Zimmer, with whom he worked on the soundtracks to both *Despicable Me* films. Over retro-futurist disco, handclaps and a scratchy funk guitar motif courtesy of long-time collaborator Brent Paschke of Spymob, Williams insisted that Marilyn, Cleopatra and Joan of Arc "don't do nothing to me". (The song also featured additional spoken vocals from Ozzy Osbourne's daughter, Kelly). As Williams explained at the time, he was standing up for difference and uniqueness: "You don't have to be a certain weight, a certain height. For me, 'she' [the so-called 'ideal woman'] doesn't have to be the statuesque American standard of what beauty is." 'Marilyn Monroe' was the second single lifted off *G I R L* (after 'Happy') in March, when it fared well in several European charts, notably Belgium and Germany.

Second track 'Brand New' featured Justin Timberlake and was a simpler celebration of, well, simplicity: "Life to me is crazy," crooned Pharrell. "People make it complicated." 'Hunter' was "written from the perspective of the girl, to me", he explained over music containing references, according to an early review in *NME*, to INXS' 'Need You Tonight', Talking Heads circa 'Once

In A Lifetime', and the Blondie of 'Rapture'. 'Gush' was a song about sex, Williams singing, "I don't know what came over me" as the music captured the classic Neptunes sound. He seemed to justify the track at the playback when he warned the press: "There are times [on the album] where I get a little bit cute. But I should be allowed to do that."

'Happy' was next, followed by 'Come Get It Bae', a duet with Miley Cyrus, bearing hints of Jamaican dancehall music, impeccable production and lyrics in which Williams enquired, "You want to ride my motorcycle?" It was released in the US as the third single from *G I R L* in May, peaking at number 23 on the *Billboard* Hot 100 (it also reached number 108 in France). 'Gust Of Wind' found Williams renewing his collaboration with Daft Punk, who also provided vocals. Apparently Pharrell's favourite track – the lyric came to him in a dream – it had a touch of James Bond drama about it, as well as some of the disco-pop euphoria of *Random Access Memories*. It was later released (in October) as the fourth single from the album, stalling at number 32 in France.

At the playback at Sony HQ, Williams prefaced 'Lost Queen' with the explanation that there would be no real music on it, "Just some tribal guys harmonising, and I sing on top of it." According to *The Guardian*'s Michael Cragg it "harks back to some of his most strikingly minimal and experimental production work on the likes of 'Drop It Like It's Hot' and 'Milkshake'". The song signalled the start of the looser, more creatively freewheeling section of the album. 'Freq' (short for "frequency") was a "hidden track", one that Williams referred to as an "interlude", although it was as long as a full track. It was built around the repeated mantra, "You gotta go inward to experience the outer space that was built for you," delivered between snatches of what sounded like a breathing exercise as Pharrell intoned, "Individuality makes life better" over crashing waves, before R&B singer JoJo joined in for a rapturously pretty Stevie Wonder-ish mid-section, including the immortal, and significant, line: "I'd rather be a freak than not be unique." 'Know Who You Are' was a skanking duet with Alicia Keys. Finally, there was 'It Girl', a shiny slice of commercial dance music that nodded to classic Michael Jackson, all glossy harmonies, crisp production and falsetto flights of fancy, with a coda that paid homage to Pharrell's beloved A Tribe Called Quest. It would be released in November as the fifth single from the album, with an anime-inspired clip featuring Williams rendered in the style of Japanese cartoons and video games.

At the end of the G I R L playback Pharrell declared to the journalists, delighted by their impressed applause: "I'm a perfectionist. But I'm really content this time. This is my most favourite work."

G I R L reached number one in 12 countries (including the UK, where it was the fastest-selling album of the year up to that point and subsequently awarded a Platinum disc for over 300,000 sales), and the Top 10 in 17 other countries. It had sold almost 600,000 copies in the US by February 2015. At the 57th Grammy Awards, it was nominated for Album of the Year and won Best Urban Contemporary Album.

Reviewers seemed to go with the commercial flow in the wake of the staggering global success of 'Get Lucky', 'Blurred Lines' and 'Happy' and gave G I R L almost unanimous praise. *Billboard* called it "a relentlessly positive and unselfconsciously joyful tour de force". AllMusic decided it was "easily Pharrell's second most enjoyable album, just behind the original version of *In Search Of...* from 2001. It's fun, frivolous, and low on excess." *Spin* awarded it eight out of 10, calling it "unabashedly feminine and neatly spaced-out" and saying: "That lighter-than-helium vibe is all over G I R L, the most audacious milestone in the Neptunes/N★E★R★D. icon's already storied career." Hip hop bible *XXL* gave the album an XL rating, and decided that it should "further his reputation as a pop icon. Let the man's hot streak continue." *Time Out* was ambivalent, declaring it, at its best, "one of the biggest and best pop albums of the year", while at its worst it resembled the curdled, creamy muzak of British easy-listening music station Magic FM. That left *Fact* magazine to sound the one truly negative note: "*G I R L* is 45 minutes of warmed-over retro-pop pastiche, cribbing from Michael Jackson and Chic, from disco and yacht rock," it wrote. "Mostly, Pharrell is content to approximate dance-floor fillers from the seventies and eighties; at his worst, he rehashes the more soulful and innovative material he made a decade ago."

Also receiving widespread acclaim around the same time as *G I R L* was the motion picture soundtrack to *The Amazing Spider-Man 2*, a further collaboration between Williams and Hans Zimmer, which was released in April 2014. Pharrell spoke about the experience with *Time Out*, and was as modest as usual.

"Hans is an amazing guy. So you know, if my only contribution was to pay for his coffee I'd be happy," he said. "But he's giving me really generous creative real estate and we're just basically filling up the canvas. I'm just really happy to be a part of it. I'm having a really good time with it."

He moved on to discuss his work with Zimmer on the Superman movie *Man Of Steel*. "I shouldn't get much credit – I was one of, like, 12 drummers who did the drum parts that Hans wrote. So it's not even like I wrote anything. I was merely part of an ensemble," he said. "He's been incredibly generous to me and my career. The most valuable part of our friendship is that he doesn't mind sharing gems about the craft with me. That's something I can never pay for. It's invaluable information."

Having worked on *Man Of Steel* and *Spider-Man 2*, the assumption was that he was a comic book fan. "I'm a semi-comic book fan," he said. "I'm a fan of Magneto [an associate of Marvel characters The X-Men]."

The *Time Out* journalist took the opportunity to ask Pharrell to survey his magnificent achievements of the past year, including the world's three biggest songs. What was his process?

"There are different ways of doing it," he replied, explaining that he got some of his best ideas in the shower, "like Einstein". "For me, I want to chase after a feeling, something that just feels good. And from there, lyrically, the music just sort of sets the template for the words. The feeling directs all creativity. The beat comes first. My job is just to listen to it, and let it tell me what should be fed lyrically, where the drums should go, where the melodies should go. It's all by feel."

Did he know which of his songs would be hits ahead of their release? "No, I don't know when a song is going to be huge – you never know, really. The people make that decision. The only thing you can do is be loyal to your creativity and try to do something new and fresh, and leave it at that. What makes a song huge is people buying records, streaming it online, voting for it, and those are things that are out of my control. Those are the factors that make a song a hit; it's never been me. The people decide. What I do is such a small part."

He credited his parents with his love of music and the freedom and confidence to pursue it as a career. "I had a mum and dad who urged me to pursue music but at the same time were realistic about it. It just sort of happened, to be honest. I can't [come up with] a special inspirational story. It's mostly my parents who didn't shoot me down when I wanted to do it. Nor did they put too much pressure on me."

Reminiscing about his initial encounter with Chad Hugo at band camp and his subsequent rapid rise in the music industry, the journalist wondered if there was ever a point where either of them realised, "We've made it!" "No, I don't have a specific moment where I thought 'I've made it'," he said. "I never look at it like that. I always looked at it like, 'Wow, I get to do it again.' You can't assume you've made it. That's too much of an assumption. I just want to work."

Pharrell had spoken about his many collaborators before, describing them generously as "giant angels who are much smarter than me, who can oversee the things that I don't know shit about". Of all the musicians Pharrell had worked with, Jay-Z was singled out in his *Time Out* interview as an example of someone "growing deeper and deeper into his comfort zone and his understanding of who he is, as an entity and his purpose on this planet. He's secure with himself. When he works, it's interesting to watch." Meanwhile, Beyoncé was "the queen", and Prince was the artist he'd most like to work with.

There was a further overview of his career on the website Stereogum, only this time it was the music scene in general that Pharrell was surveying. He described *Pure Heroine*, the debut album by fast-rising teenage New Zealander Lorde, as "genius from front to back; bookend to bookend. Lorde is a phenomenal, phenomenal artist." Also "genius" was the album *good kid, m.A.A.d city* by rapper Kendrick Lamar. "And I was lucky enough to be a part of it [on the track 'good kid'], but his album – aside from my song – is genius in itself. Lyrically, to me, he's just one of the best." Drake, too, was singled out – "I think Drake is masterful with his work" – as was Tyler, The Creator ("He is in a really good place right now") and Taylor Swift ("She has mastered her audience and what it is that she loves to do. You can say whatever you want, but they're great lyrics, and she knows what her audience wants and she knows that good feeling").

Following *G I R L*, 'Blurred Lines', *Random Access Memories*, 'Happy' and the rest of his furious output of 2013-14, Pharrell hardly rested on his laurels. There was a flurry of activity, covering as many areas of artistry and creativity as Pharrell could manage. He saw 'Sing', his latest co-composition and production, sung by Ed Sheeran, become the ginger British troubadour's first number one UK single and first us Top 20 hit. There was a book deal inked with Putnam, a subsidiary of Penguin, to write four children's books, including a picture book inspired by his huge solo hit. A 250,000-copy run of *Happy*, the book, was due to be published on September 22, 2015, and would feature photographs of children from around the world "celebrating what it means to be happy".

"I'm humbled by the global success of 'Happy', but especially in awe of the song's young fans," Pharrell said in a statement. "My collaboration with Penguin allows me to continue a dialogue with these children in a fresh, new way. We're both committed to feeding the curiosity of young minds with imagination."

In May 2014, Williams curated an art show named after his album *G I R L* at the Galerie Perrotin in Paris, France. The show included 37 artists such as Takashi Murakami, JR, Daniel Arsham and Marina Abramović. He contributed to rapper Azealia Banks' long-awaited debut album, *Broke With Expensive Taste*, although his song, 'ATM Jam', didn't make the final cut. Williams was the executive producer of T.I.'s ninth studio album, *Paperwork*. The Dear G I R L tour of Europe, in support of *G I R L,* was Williams' first solo tour since 2006, and began in Istanbul in September 2014. Comme des Garçons developed a unisex fragrance with Williams, with artist KAWS designing the bottle.

In January 2015, the unlikely combination of Pharrell Williams and Al Gore announced what they hoped would be the largest global campaign in history, in the form of a second round of Live Earth concerts (after the 2007 ones) to promote awareness of climate change. The concerts were due to take place across all seven continents – including Antarctica – on June 18. Williams, mooted to be the musical director, spoke at the World Economic Forum in Davos about the event aiming for a global television audience of two billion across 193 television networks. "Instead of just having people perform, we literally are going to have humanity harmonise all at once," he said, vaguely.

Williams recalled the first Live Earth in Rio de Janeiro in 2007, describing it as "a ball". However, he said, "You would have pundits and comedians who didn't understand global warming and we were often ridiculed. We wanted to do something very different this time."

Event producer Kevin Wall said: "The power of music is unique, because it's borderless, without language. Pharrell will use that power. When you combine music with a message, you can effect change."

As though to confirm that he could tune in to the politics of the moment, at the 2015 Grammy Awards Williams performed an orchestral rendition of 'Happy' with composer Hans Zimmer and pianist Lang Lang that included a tribute to the Black Lives Matter "Hands Up, Don't Shoot" movement inspired by Eric Garner's death and the killing of Michael Brown in Ferguson, Missouri.

From the serious to the sublimely silly, in February 2015, Williams made a cameo in an episode of *The Simpsons* entitled *Walking Big & Tall*, in which he came to Springfield to write a new anthem for the town. Also on a cartoon/animation tip in 2015, Williams contributed three songs to the soundtrack of *The SpongeBob Movie: Sponge Out of Water*, and one – 'Shine', with Gwen Stefani – for *Paddington*. In June 2015, he was scheduled to be one of the headliners at the highly prestigious Glastonbury festival, along with Mary J Blige, Motörhead, Patti Smith, Foo Fighters and Kanye West.

By 2015, the rapper, producer, songwriter, fashion designer, *Voice* coach and mogul was estimated to be worth around $80 million. He was also by now a major philanthropist – as part of his bid to "teach kids to fish", he was running a charity called From One Hand To AnOTHER, a foundation that assists at-risk youths between the ages of seven and 20 in communities throughout America. "The simplest way to say it is that I think we're all dealt these cards in life, but the cards in and of themselves don't read one way or the other," he said. "It's up to you to home in on and cultivate whatever you've got in your hand. Most of the time, I see what I see, I search my feelings, and then I make my decisions based on my gut – and I don't always make the right ones."

The ever-active yet strangely ageless polymath offered an insight into his daily routine. He rose around 9am, and the first thing he did was pray. "First thing I do is thank the master. I thank God every day." Then he went in the shower – the site of many fresh ideas – after which he spent between 10.30am and 12 noon on the phone. After that, he entered the recording studio, between 12 and 1. "I work from 1 or 2-ish to maybe 9 or 11 every day," he explained.

A typical night involved watching the news or the Discovery Channel, or perhaps some "esoteric aliens stuff". Bedtime was between midnight and 2am.

His busy schedule reflected an innate desire to keep moving. "I can't get stuck doing only one thing," he said. "I have to work with different people doing different things. It's where my energy comes from. I am inspired by life in general: conversations, movies, reactions to things, everything."

The multimillionaire superstar who grew up in the projects of Virginia Beach wearing Led Zeppelin T-shirts and playing drums in a hip hop band was now in charge of an organisation with headquarters in New York and satellite offices in Miami and Los Angeles. "I've always been the kid who didn't fit in the box," he said.

Did he get lucky? Far from it. This was destiny. "I used to say, 'Me? Really? Okay, cool!' But then when I looked over my shoulder, I could see that there was a clear path. Someone might say that Teddy Riley building his studio five minutes from my high school was luck. I mean, why leave New York and go there? But I don't see that now."

For Williams, being shrewd and discerning was key to his success, a success that, a quarter of a century after the Neptunes' first studio sessions, saw no sign of abating. "Existence is all mathematics, and I see it as me listening to the math that is right in front of me. There's a key for every door, and if you can't find it, you can make one. That's always an option."

Above all, any decisions he made were designed to maintain a calm mind. By the time his head hit the pillow at night, he was happy.

"I never feel anxious about anything," he revealed. "Why would I? If I felt anxious or put pressure on myself then nothing would be fun."

DAFT PUNK
A Trip Inside the Pyramid
Dina Santolleri

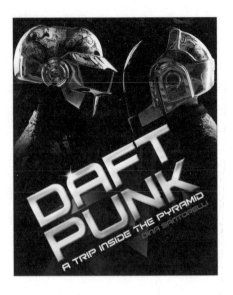

Daft Punk: A Trip Inside the Pyramid is the first book to pull together the complete story of the lives and work of Grammy award-winning Thomas Bangalter and Guy-Manuel de Homem-Christo, the French musicians behind the legendary robot masks. Chronicling Daft Punk's earliest musical and artistic influences – as diverse as Barry Manilow, Giorgio Moroder, Kraftwerk and even Andy Warhol – to their rise to international superstardom, this book delves deep into the Daft Punk discography, weaving together the history of electronic dance music and the culture surrounding it.

A Trip Inside the Pyramid follows every step of the duo's career, from the origin of the robot personas to their brilliant live shows, and explores the making of each album – including the newest sounds on *Random Access Memories* – as well as the tiers of collaborators who have revelled in the opportunity to work with this iconic duo.

Daft Punk's enduring legacy permeates the world of electronic dance music. Filled with rare photos, insights and revelations, this book explains why.

Dina Santolleri has been a freelance writer for more than fifteen years and has written frequently about entertainment and pop culture topics. Dina serves as the executive editor of Salute and Family magazines, for which she has interviewed many celebrities. She has collaborated on a variety of book projects and is a lecturer for Hofstra University's continuing education department. For more information about Dina, visit her website at www.dinasantolleri.com.

Available from **www.omnibuspress.com**

ISBN: 978.1.84938.699.9
Order No: OP53867